ARISTOTLE POETICS

ARISTOTLE
POETICS

TRANSLATED
WITH AN INTRODUCTION AND NOTES
BY
GERALD F. ELSE

ANN ARBOR PAPERBACKS
THE UNIVERSITY OF MICHIGAN PRESS

CONTENTS

INTRODUCTION

Aristotle and Literature

Aristotle was a doctor's son and retained a lifelong interest in anatomy and physiology; had an analytical mind so acute, so fertile in questions, distinctions, definitions, arguments, objections, and solutions, that his fellow students in the Academy are said to have dubbed him The Brain (*noûs*); was well read and especially enjoyed the theater, but in a somewhat old-fashioned way, tending to put Sophocles and Euripides above the newer dramatists, although some of the latter were good friends of his; was bored and a little shocked by Aristophanes but thrilled again and again, all his life, by the dramatic genius of Homer, whom he considered the perfect poet of all time; wrote verses occasionally, in tribute to a beloved friend or for other purposes of that kind, though he had little feeling for the magic of words and none for any religious or metaphysical dimension in poetry; was on the whole a conservative and conventional-minded professional man with special competence in the sciences: anything but a literary type—.

It seems at first blush only middling equipment for one who was to become—much, much later, to be sure —a czar of literary criticism. And indeed one cannot help wondering what it was that impelled Aristotle to

include a course in the theory of literature among the
lectures he gave to the graduate students of his Lyceum.
For that is what our *Poetics* is: a lecture script (or rather,
as we shall see, part of one). He hardly did it merely in
order to complete the building of what we call the Aris-
totelian system, or to become the master of *color che
sanno*. And not because literature so obsessed and trou-
bled him that he could not leave it alone. It is in fact
almost certain that Aristotle would never have con-
structed a theory of literature, or in any case would not
have ended with the one he did, if he had not begun his
intellectual career as a pupil of Plato.

Plato, Poetry, and the Academy

Plato, unlike his brightest pupil, was a man obsessed,
hounded, by poetry and poets all his life. Tradition says
that he wrote dithyrambs and tragedies when he was
very young, but destroyed them after he met Socrates.
It does not matter whether the story is true or only *ben
trovato*. One has to do no more than skim the *Protagoras*
or the *Charmides* or the *Symposium* to be aware of a lit-
erary and dramatic talent equal to any in the world's
roster. (A comic talent and temperament, however, more
than a tragic. Plato is more like Aristophanes than he is
like any tragic poet. The affinity peeps out unabashed,
to the possible discomfiture of soberer-minded Platonists,
in the *Symposium*.)

Actually, Plato was a multiple genius, with quite
other talents besides those for poetry and drama. He was
in fact an incredible rarity: a blue-blooded aristocrat,
born to rule, who also had supreme intellectual, aesthetic,
and spiritual endowments. When he gave up everything

else for Socrates, that is, for "philosophy," it was a total commitment, a sacrifice out of proportion to those which are made every day by slighter and colder souls: the kind that are appropriately known as "career decisions."

The fascination that Plato felt all his life for great poetry—for Homer, Alcaeus, Anacreon, Simonides, Aeschylus, Sophocles, and all the rest—was in part sensuous, for he possessed in great measure what Aristotle lacked, the sense of word, rhythm, musical phrase, style. But it was also, in the highest sense of those (Greek) words, political and ethical. Plato felt in the great poets, and above all in Homer, the Homer of the *Iliad*, the pull of a way of life, a claim on the allegiance of men, a norm for living, which still had meaning and attractiveness for his contemporaries. Plato heard that siren call more clearly than any of them; but against it he pitted the apocalyptic truth he had learned from Socrates, that only goodness exists and has power. All the appearances of this world, all its temptations to believe in evil, are of no avail once a man has grasped this truth and taken it into himself. But the poets do not know the truth. They present a world in which evil is real and potent, in which great men suffer and are defeated for no sufficient reason, in which the gods are hostile or at best indifferent to man's faring. Therefore the poets must be fought and conquered, so that their teaching may be countered in men's souls.

This apocalyptic faith—the necessity of a struggle to the death against the poets for the soul of Greece—is the true background of what we conventionally call Plato's "literary criticism." It alone explains the famous ostracism of the poets from the good State. We need not doubt Plato's own protestations of love for Homer and the tragedians; but great is the truth and it must prevail.

The banishment of the poets is justified by two main accusations, the one ideological, the other moral, which are rehearsed in Book 10 of the *Republic*: (1) they are *imitators* of things, at two removes from reality, and (2) they cater to our emotions, i.e., the un- and anti-rational part of our nature, especially its tendencies to *pity and fear*.

When Aristotle came to the Academy to begin his studies in 367, the charge against the poets and its two crucial points, "imitation" and "pity and fear," were already, as we should say, a part of the historical record (the *Republic* was written in the 370's). It is no accident that these very concepts, "imitation" and "pity and fear," are at the heart of the *Poetics*. At the end of his renewed attack on the poets in Book 10 of the *Republic*, Plato invites anybody who is equipped and minded to do so to step up to the bar and defend poetry. The *Poetics* is a brief for that defense.

Aristotle and the Defense of Poetry

Not in form; for this is not a court in which an ordinary plea of defense would be entertained. The defense attorney must show *what poetry is and what it can do*; in short, he must bring in evidence a viable philosophy of literature.

Aristotle was able to do this precisely because for him poetry was not the Adversary, the Other Way of Life, but simply a valid presentation, within its own sphere and by its own appropriate means, of certain truths about human beings and the way they act. Any claim that it has a higher truth to offer, an insight into God or Fate or the Nature of Things, is tacitly waived before the case is called for trial. Poetry is more philosophical than history, but it is not philosophy. In Aristotle's analysis of tragedy (and epic) there is an element called Thought, but it has to do with the arguments and general ideas presented by the characters in the course of their action, not with any view of the world possessed by the poet; if he has one, it is apparently no concern of the critic and no determinative element in his own art.

There was another idea of poetry which had appeared from time to time in Plato's works (*Ion, Symposium, Phaedrus*), only to disappear again: the idea of Inspiration. According to this conception, poetry is not a mere earthly activity but a winged creature inspired by God, or the gods. Surely this cannot be overlooked in any thorough defense of poetry? Whatever the reason (and to my notion the status of poetic Inspiration had been oblique and precarious even in Plato's thinking), Aristotle does not in fact make any significant use of the idea. There is one passing reference to poetic madness, in section 17; but however interpreted, it clearly does not belong to the main structure of Aristotle's theory.

Plato had alleged, then, that the poet was a mere imitator, without access to reality and truth. For him, of course, "reality and truth" meant the Ideas, especially the Idea of the Good. Aristotle, as is well known, rejected the Platonic Ideas. Hence, when he describes the poet as an imitator of an action begun and finished by human beings, he is not debarring him from access to any pertinent reality. Human life is an entity of practical nature and relevance; it has no metaphysical dimension.

(Individual human beings can of course turn away from ordinary human activities and devote themselves to pure contemplation; but that is another order of existence altogether.) When the poet "imitates" human action, therefore, he is imitating something very real and direct, and if he has any experience of life and any poetic (=dramatic) talent he can give us a valuable extension of our ordinary experience. Thus, whereas for Plato "imitation" had been a self-defeating, sterile activity, for Aristotle it is a positive and fruitful one—within its allowed limits.

A similar peripety appears to overtake the emotions of pity and fear. Plato had seen them as negative and menacing, an encouragement to indulgence in our natural passions. What Aristotle thinks about them is not entirely clear in the extant portion of the *Poetics*, but so much is clear, that he considers them both natural and desirable emotional tendencies. The question is not whether they shall be aroused but how they shall be handled.

A note on "catharsis" seems to be unavoidable here. The term appears just once in the extant part of the *Poetics* (sec. 9, 1449b28), and then not in a context that offers a firm handle to interpretation. We are hindered rather than helped by another concept, that of the "appropriate (or specific) pleasure," which is clearly said at one point (sec. 14, 1453b12) to be based somehow on pity and fear, but whose relationship to "catharsis" is left wholly obscure. The most that can be said with confidence—and this much *can* be said with confidence —is that "catharsis" belongs in some way to Aristotle's defense of the emotional side of poetry against Plato. The arousing of pity and fear is an integral part of the

work of tragedy, at least, and something about that pro-
duction is such that those feelings are, or can be made,
beneficent rather than hurtful. In any case—and perhaps
this is the most important thing in the long run—it is
clear that Aristotle accepts, nay insists on, an emotional
as well as an intellectual side of poetry.

In more than one way, Aristotle in his role of de-
fender of poetry can be taken not merely as the voice of
reason and good sense but as spokesman for the Greek na-
tion, vindicating the treasures of its great literature against
Plato's devastating but one-sided attack. Yet the position is
not wholly restored. For all his good will and good sense,
Aristotle could not and did not vindicate one profoundly
important aspect of the greatest Greek literature: its
religious dimension. For better or worse, Aristotle is a
fourth-century intellectual, and one trained by Plato at
that. He no more believed in the gods of his fathers than
we do, and he was quite blind to the religious depths not
only of Sophocles or Aeschylus but also of Homer and
Euripides. In Aristotle's world, poetry is an entirely
secular activity.

Perhaps that deficiency is what made it possible for
the *Poetics* to become eventually a literary Bible for
Renaissance classicism: it contained no Hellenic pieties
that might have conflicted with Christian dogma or
wounded Christian sensibilities. By the same token, how-
ever, we cannot accept it as a satisfactory account of all
Greek poetry, much less as a valid guide to all literature.
There are some things, and very important things, that
are not dreamt of in Aristotle's philosophy.

But though his treatise must be declared ultimately
deficient, what it does tell us is not often wrong. Aris-
totle's analytical eye has caught most of the truth about

the structures and main procedures of Greek poetry. Kept in close and sympathetic reciprocal relationship with the literature it interprets, the treatise has invaluable insights to offer.

The *Poetics* Among the Works of Aristotle

The *Poetics*, as was said above, is a set of lecture notes. As such it belongs to the large group of "acroamatic" works which are all that we have left, except for fragments, of Aristotle's total production. These works were the outgrowth of courses given in his school, the Lyceum (founded in 335 B.C.), and/or of similar courses given by him previously in the Academy itself (before Plato's death in 347), at Assos in the Troad, and perhaps at Pella in Macedonia when Aristotle was there as tutor-in-chief to the young Alexander (342-335). They remained essentially in and of the school: "esoteric" in that sense, though not in the sense of harboring any secret doctrine taught only to initiates.

Aristotle was much better known in antiquity, at least during the two to three centuries after his death, for his published or "exoteric" works. Mostly in dialogue form, these productions belonged chiefly to his earlier years, before he founded the Lyceum, and were praised for their graceful, at times impressive style (difficult as that is to believe after much immersion in the *Poetics*). In form, the dialogues were more like Plato's later than his earlier, "Socratic" dialogues: a systematic, scientific discussion carried on by Aristotle and/or some of his colleagues. We can get an idea of their nature, perhaps also of their tone, from the dialogues of Cicero, which were explicitly modeled on Aristotle's.

Among the dialogues was a relatively long (three books) and, it would appear, important one *On Poets*. This is almost certainly the "published discourses" alluded to at the beginning of section 17 (end of old chapter 15). It has been studied with particular care by Rostagni (see Bibliography, p. 115). From some citations and from references to the dialogue it is apparent that a number of the leading ideas of the *Poetics* were anticipated in it, and that if we possessed it our task in interpreting the treatise would be considerably lightened.

The word "anticipated" was used just now simply because the dialogues belonged or are believed to have belonged, *as a whole*, to an earlier period than the acroamatic works. But there must have been some overlapping. The *Poetics* is usually assigned to the Lyceum period, after 335, but without discussion and for no better reason than that that is the traditional date for acroamatic works. When one considers Aristotle's presumable reason for dealing with poetry at all, as set forth above, it seems likely on the contrary that he would have begun much earlier, before—perhaps long before—Plato's death. A not implausible date might be 360–355 (we know that the earliest parts of Aristotle's *Rhetoric* go back to this period). Moreover, we have absolutely no way of knowing which work, the dialogue or the treatise, preceded the other; they may well have been contemporaneous. Finally, the state of the *Poetics* text is compatible with the conjecture that Aristotle may have abandoned the subject at an early date, perhaps turning it over to younger colleagues like Dicaearchus or Aristoxenus who were then "working in the field."

The Text of the *Poetics*

Whatever the reason, the text of the *Poetics* is abrupt, elliptical, sometimes incoherent, to a degree unexampled among Aristotle's other acroamatic works. The two groups of works underwent a number of vicissitudes after his death. According to a well-known story which has been unduly doubted, the acroamatic treatises were lost for two centuries or more after Aristotle's death, during which time he was known only by the published works, and did not come to light again until the first century B.C. Subsequently, owing apparently at least in part to the false idea that the acroamatic works contained the "real," secret doctrine, they were copied and intensively studied while the published works, including the one *On Poets*, were neglected and ultimately lost; so that the older situation was exactly reversed.

During this period of renewed activity upon the acroamatic works, the *Poetics* obviously survived. But only one half of it survived; for it was most likely then that its second book was lost (we know from evidence both internal and external that the *Poetics* originally had two books). Moreover, the work seems to have been little known to the Aristotelian commentators of the third to fifth centuries A.D., some of whom were admirably learned men—unless indeed they deliberately ignored it; in any case they hardly ever quote from it. What is more, *no commentary was ever written on the Poetics* (which means incidentally that it never had the benefit, which most of the other acroamatic works enjoyed, of having its text checked and reviewed by competent scholars); and when the torso ultimately survived into the Middle Ages it seems to have done so not as a part of the Aristotelian corpus but as one of a mixed bag of rhetorical treatises by various authors: so in manuscript A (see below).

The next firm item in the history of the *Poetics* text is that it arrived in Italy, as a part of A, sometime not long after the middle of the fifteenth century, as is attested by the fact that copies began to be made then; more than thirty are known in all. Its influence, however, was slow in spreading. A Latin translation by Giorgio Valla was published in 1498, the Greek text in 1508 (from a copy of A and, characteristically enough, as part of the Aldine *Rhetores Graeci*). The commentaries by Robortello, Vettori (Victorius), Castelvetro, and the rest, which established Aristotle as the dictator of criticism, did not begin until well into the sixteenth century, and of course French classicism reached its apogee only in the seventeenth. In Paris around 1660, when Racine studied the *Poetics* with respectful care, the story had come more than full circle: the little work which had lain unknown or neglected for the first two or three centuries of its existence and then had almost been lost again, in later antiquity, now rose to such despotic power that great poets—for example, Corneille—lived in awe and dread of its supposedly infallible "rules." The total sequence of events, including this final peripety *eis eutychian*, might have drawn an ironical smile from Aristotle if he had lived to witness it.

Manuscripts, Editions, Commentaries

We now know—subject to new discoveries—that we have four independent witnesses to the *Poetics* text:

A,   *Parisinus graecus 1741*, tenth or eleventh century;

B,   *Riccardianus 46*, twelfth century;

Lat., represented by *Etonensis 129* and *Toletanus 47.10:*
       A.D. 1278, Latin translation by Wm. of Moerbeke
       from a lost original;

Ar.,   *Paris. gr. arab. 2346*, tenth century:
       Arabic translation by Abu bišr Matta from a lost
       Syriac translation of a lost Greek original.

The new Oxford Classical Text edition of the
Poetics by Rudolf Kassel (1965) makes all previous edi-
tions obsolete, being the only one that provides any-
thing like full and accurate reports from all four text
witnesses. The best previous editions, *qua* editions, were
those of Butcher, Sykutris, and Rostagni; the best com-
mentaries, besides the ones just mentioned (Butcher's
essays practically constitute a commentary), those of
Bywater and Valgimigli. A warning must be sounded
against both the text and commentary of Gudeman, as
being uncritical and unreliable.

Modern Translations of the *Poetics*

The most influential translations in English, and always
worth comparing if the student wants a close reading of
a difficult passage, have been those of Butcher and By-
water. Unfortunately, Bywater's translation was made
from a Greek text that was behind the times even when
it was first published in 1898. The version by Grube is
also worth consulting, as is the French of Hardy. A
German translation with notes is promised by Kassel, the
Oxford editor; it should be an important work.
    The present translation is based on Kassel's text. It

was worked out, to begin with, quite independently of the one, or ones, published in my book on the *Poetics* (1957), then compared with the earlier versions throughout. The new translation is still on the literal side. I have striven for English idiom but not for elegance (which would give a positively misleading idea of the style of the *Poetics*). The one respect in which I have consistently departed from literalness is in *expanding* phrases, clauses, or sentences for the sake of clarity, where the ground for such expansion is certain. Most often this consists in spelling out a subject, a predicate, or whatever, which Aristotle has left for the reader—that is, himself, most likely—to supply. Bywater (p. v) confessed to having "not scrupled . . . to insert here and there words or short clauses, in order to make the sense and sequence of ideas clearer—as I suppose Aristotle would have done himself, if he had foreseen the modern reader." I have not scrupled to do the same. On the other hand I have refrained from doing something else that Bywater admits doing, namely "to recast many of Aristotle's sentences." I have tried on the contrary to keep them as they are, even when they get long and tedious by modern standards. I presuppose a reader with some concern not only for the matter but the manner of Aristotle's treatment.

The translation, faithful as it is or tries to be, reflects many ideas and points of interpretation which I arrived at long ago and which run counter to accepted readings of the *Poetics*. Many though by no means all of these are mentioned in the notes; whether they are or not, arguments for almost all of them will be found in my book *Aristotle's Poetics: The Argument* (Cambridge, Mass.: Harvard University Press, 1957). Attentive stu-

dents who are interested in such minutiae will find some
—not many—places where I have tacitly withdrawn or
modified an interpretation advanced in that book. On
the other hand I have tried to play fair with the reader
by calling explicit attention, in a note, to every place
(except for very minor variants such as the number
of a noun) where the Greek text I have translated differs
from that of Kassel.

Note on Section and Page Numbering

The section numbers in the center of the page are partly
new, through no. 12; from no. 13 on, with minor excep-
tions, they coincide with the traditional chapter num-
bering. The latter is also shown throughout the work,
in square brackets.

The references in the left-hand margin follow the
system universally employed in citing works of Aristotle.
The *Poetics* occupies pages 1447 (often shortened in
references to 47) through 1462 in the second volume of
the edition of Aristotle prepared for the Berlin Academy
by Immanuel Bekker (1830). The letters a and b signify
left- and right-hand columns respectively. Thus, the
reference 51a12 means: page 1451, left-hand column,
line 12 in Bekker.

POETICS

1 [1]

Basic considerations

1447a8   The art of poetic composition¹ in general
and its various species, the function and effect
of each of them; how the plots should be con-
10   structed | if the composition is to be an artistic
success; how many other component elements
are involved in the process, and of what kind;
and similarly all the other questions that fall
under this same branch of inquiry—these are
the problems we shall discuss; let us begin in
the right and natural way, with basic prin-
ciples.

Epic composition, then; the writing of
tragedy, and of comedy also; the composing
15   of dithyrambs; and the greater part of the |
making of music with flute and lyre: these
are all in point of fact, taken collectively, imi-
tative processes.² They differ from each other,
however, in three ways, namely by virtue of
having (1) different means, (2) different ob-
jects, and (3) different methods of imitation.

15

2

The differentiation according to medium

First, in the same way that certain people
imitate a variety of things by means of shapes
and colors, making visible replicas of them
20   (some doing this ¦ on the basis of art, others
out of habit), while another group produces
its mimicry with the voice, so in the case of
the arts we just mentioned: they all carry on
their imitation through the media of rhythm,
speech, and melody, but with the latter two[3]
used separately or together. Thus the arts of
25   flute and lyre music, and any | others of sim-
ilar nature and effect such as the art of the
panpipe, produce their imitation using melody
and rhythm alone,[4] while there is another[5]
which does so using speeches[6] or verses alone,
29 | 47b8   bare of music, and | either mixing the verses
with one another or employing just one cer-
tain kind—an art which is, as it happens, name-
10   less up to the present time. In fact | we could
not even assign a common name to the mimes
of Sophron and Xenarchus and the Socratic
discourses;[7] nor again if somebody should
compose his imitation in trimeters or elegiac
couplets or certain other verses of that kind;[8]
(Except[9] people do link up poetic composition
with verse and speak of "elegiac poets," "epic
15   poets," not treating them | as poets by virtue
of their imitation, but employing the term as
a common appellation going along with the
use of verse. And in fact the name is also

applied to anyone who treats a medical or scientific topic in verses, yet Homer and Empedocles[10] actually have nothing in common except their verse; hence the proper term for the one is "poet," for the other, "science-

20 writer" rather than | "poet.") and likewise if someone should mix all the kinds of verse[11] together in composing his imitation, as Chaeremon composed a *Centaur* using all the verses.[12]

Such is the disjunction we feel is called for in these cases. There are on the other hand certain arts which use all the aforesaid | media,

25 I mean such as rhythm, song, and verse.[13] The composition of dithyrambs and of nomes does so, and both tragedy and comedy. But there is a difference in that some of these arts use all the media at once while others use them in different parts of the work.

These then are the differentiations of the poetic arts with respect to the media in which

29 the poets carry on their imitation. |

3 [2]
The objects of imitation

| 48a1   Since those who imitate imitate men in action,[14] and these must necessarily be either worthwhile or worthless people[15] (for definite characters tend pretty much to develop in men of action),[16] it follows that they imitate[17] men either better or worse than the average,

5 | as the painters do—for Polygnotus used to portray superior and Pauson inferior men;[18]

and it is evident that each of the forms of
imitation aforementioned will include these
differentiations, that is, will differ by virtue
of imitating objects which are different in this
sense. Indeed it is possible for these dissimilari-
10 ties to turn up | in flute and lyre playing,[19]
and also in prose dialogues and bare verses:
thus Homer imitated superior men[20] and
Hegemon of Thasos, the inventor of parody,
and Nicochares, the author of the *Deiliad*,[21]
inferior ones; likewise in connection with
15 dithyrambs and | nomes, for one can make
the imitation the way Timotheus and Philoxe-
nus did their Cyclopes.[22] Finally, the difference
between tragedy and comedy coincides exactly
with the master-difference: namely the one
tends to imitate people better, the other one
people worse, than the average.

4 [3]
The modes of imitation

The third way of differentiating these
20 arts is by the mode | of imitation. For it is
possible to imitate the same objects, and in
the same media, (1) by narrating part of the
time and dramatizing the rest of the time,[23]
which is the way Homer composes[24] (mixed
mode), or (2) with the same person continu-
ing without change (straight narrative), or
(3) with all the persons who are performing
the imitation[25] acting, that is, carrying on for
themselves (straight dramatic mode).

5
*Jottings, chiefly on comedy*²⁶

Poetic imitation, then, shows these three
25 *differentiae*, | as we said at the beginning: in
the media, objects, and modes of imitation. So
in one way Sophocles would be the same
(kind of) imitator as Homer, since they both
imitate worthwhile people, and in another
way the same as Aristophanes, for they both
imitate people engaged in action, doing things.²⁷
In fact some authorities maintain that that is
why plays are called dramas, because the imi-
tation is of men acting (*dróntas*, from *drân*,
30 'do, act'). It is also the reason why | both
tragedy and comedy are claimed by the Dor-
ians: comedy by the Megarians, both those
from hereabouts, who say that it came into
being during the period of their democracy,
and those in Sicily,²⁸ and tragedy by some |
35 of those in the Peloponnese.²⁹ They use the
names "comedy" and "drama"³⁰ as evidence;
for they say that *they* call their outlying vil-
lages *kômai* while the Athenians call theirs
"demes" (*dêmoi*)—the assumption being that
the participants in comedy were called
kômôidoi not from their being revelers but
because they wandered from one village to
another, being degraded and excluded from the
38 | 48b1 city— | and that they call "doing" or "acting"
drân while the Athenians designate it by *prat-
tein*.³¹

6
The origin and development of poetry

So much, then, for the *differentiae* of im-
[4]
itation, their number and identity. As to
the origin of the poetic art as a whole, it stands
5   to reason that two | operative causes brought
it into being, both of them rooted in human
nature. Namely (1) the habit of imitating is
congenital to human beings from childhood
(actually man differs from the other animals
in that he is the most imitative and learns his
first lessons through imitation), and so is (2)
the pleasure that all men take in works of imita-
10   tion. A proof of this is what happens | in our
experience. There are things which we see
with pain so far as they themselves are con-
cerned but whose images, even when executed
in very great detail, we view with pleasure.
Such is the case for example with renderings
of the least favored animals, or of cadavers.[32]
The cause of this also is that learning is emi-
nently pleasurable not only to philosophers
but to the rest of mankind in the same way,
15   although their share | in the pleasure is re-
stricted. For the reason they take pleasure in
seeing the images is that in the process of view-
ing they find themselves learning, that is,
reckoning what kind a given thing belongs
to: "This individual is a So-and-so."[33] Because
if the viewer happens not to have seen such a
thing before, the reproduction will not pro-

duce the pleasure *qua* reproduction but
through its workmanship or color or some-
thing else of that sort. |

20   Since, then, imitation comes naturally to
us, and melody and rhythm too (it is obvious
that verses are segments of the respective
rhythms),[34] in the beginning it was those who
were most gifted in these respects who, de-
veloping them little by little, brought the
making of poetry into being out of improvisa-
tions. And the poetic enterprise split into two
branches, in accordance with the two kinds
25   of character. | Namely, the soberer spirits
were imitating noble actions and the actions
of noble persons, while the cheaper ones were
imitating those of the worthless, producing
lampoons and invectives at first just as the
other sort were producing hymns and encomia.
(28-30)32   (. . .)[35] In them (i.e., the invectives), in ac-
cordance with what is suitable and fitting,
iambic verse also put in its appearance; indeed
that is why it is called "iambic" now, because
it is the verse in which they used to "iambize,"
that is, lampoon, each other.[36] And so some
of the early poets became composers[37] of epic,
the others of iambic, verses.

<28   <Now it happens that we cannot name
anyone before Homer as the author of that
kind of poem (i.e., an iambic poem), though it
stands to reason that there were many who
were; but from Homer on | we can do so:
thus his *Margites* and other poems of that
30>   sort.> However, just as on the serious side

35 Homer was | most truly a poet,[38] since he
was the only one who not only composed well
but constructed dramatic imitations, so too he
was the first to adumbrate the forms of comedy
by producing a (1) dramatic presentation,
and not of invective but of (2) the ludicrous.

38 | 49a1 For as the *Iliad* stands | in relation to our
tragedies, so the *Margites* stands in relation to
our comedies.

Once tragedy and comedy had been par-
tially brought to light,[39] those who were out
in pursuit of the two kinds of poetic activity,
in accordance with their own respective na-
tures, became in the one case comic poets
5 instead of | iambic poets, in the other case
producers of tragedies instead of epics, because
these genres were higher and more esteemed
than the others. Now to review the question
whether even tragedy is adequate to the basic
forms or not—a question which[40] is (can be)
judged both by itself, in the abstract, and in
relationship to our theater audiences—that
is another story.[41] However that may be, it
10 did spring from an | improvisational begin-
ning (both it and comedy: the one from
those who led off the dithyramb, the other
from those who did so for the phallic perform-
ances [?][42] which still remain on the program
in many of our cities); it did expand gradually,
each feature being further developed as it
appeared; and after it had gone through a
15 number of phases | it stopped upon attaining
its full natural growth.[43] Thus Aeschylus was

the first to expand the troupe of assisting actors
from one to two,[44] shorten the choral parts,
and see to it that the dialogue takes first place;
(18–21)   (...)[45] at the same time the verse became iambic
trimeter instead of trochaic tetrameter. For
in the beginning they used the tetrameter be-
cause the form of composition was "satyr-
like," that is, more given over to dancing,[46]
but when speech came along the very nature
of the case turned up the appropriate verse.
25   For iambic is the most speech-like | of verses.
An indication of this is that we speak more
iambics than any other kind of verse in our
conversation with each other, whereas we utter
hexameters rarely, and when we do we aban-
don the characteristic tone-pattern of ordinary
speech.

Further, as to plurality of episodes and
the other additions which are recorded as
30   having been made to tragedy, | let our account
stop here; for no doubt it would be burden-
some to record them in detail.

7 [5]
Comedy

Comedy is as we said it was, an imitation
of persons who are inferior; not, however, go-
ing all the way to full villainy, but imitating
the ugly, of which the ludicrous is one part.
35   The ludicrous, that is, is a failing | or a piece
of ugliness which causes no pain or destruc-
tion; thus, to go no farther, the comic mask

is something ugly and distorted but painless.

Now the stages of development of trag-
edy, and the men who were responsible for
them, have not escaped notice, but comedy
38 | 49b1 did escape notice in the beginning | because it
was not taken seriously. (In fact it was late
in its history that the presiding magistrate of-
ficially "granted a chorus" to the comic poets;
until then they were volunteers.) Thus com-
edy already possessed certain defining char-
acteristics when the first "comic poets," so-
called, appear in the record. Who gave it
5 masks, or prologues, or | troupes of actors
and all that sort of thing, is not known. The
composing of plots[47] came originally from
Sicily; of the Athenian poets, Crates was the
first to abandon the lampooning mode and
compose arguments, that is, plots, of a general
nature.

8
Epic and tragedy

Well then, epic poetry followed in the
wake of tragedy[48] up to the point of being
10 a (1) good-sized | (2) imitation (3) in verse
(4) of people who are to be taken seriously; but
in its having its verse unmixed with any other
and being narrative in character, there they
differ. Further, so far as its length is concerned
tragedy tries as hard as it can to exist[49] during
a single daylight period, or to vary but little,
while the epic is not limited in its time and so

15 differs in that respect. Yet | originally they
used to do this in tragedies just as much as
they did in epic poems.

The constituent elements are partly iden-
tical and partly limited to tragedy. Hence any-
body who knows about good and bad tragedy
knows about epic also; for the elements that
the epic possesses appertain to tragedy as well,
but those of tragedy are not all found in the |
20 epic.

9 [6]
Tragedy and its six constituent elements[50]

Our discussions of imitative poetry in hex-
ameters, and of comedy, will come later;[51] at
present let us deal with tragedy, recovering
from what has been said so far the definition
of its essential nature, as it was in develop-
ment. Tragedy, then, is a process of imitating
25 an action which has serious implications, | is
complete, and possesses magnitude; by means
of language which has been made sensuously
attractive, with each of its varieties found
separately in the parts; enacted by the persons
themselves and not presented through narra-
tive; through a course of pity and fear com-
pleting the purification of tragic acts which
have those emotional characteristics.[52] By "lan-
guage made sensuously attractive" I mean lan-
guage that has rhythm and melody, and by "its
30 varieties found | separately" I mean the fact
that certain parts of the play are carried on

through spoken verses alone and others the
other way round, through song.

Now first of all, since they perform the
imitation through action (by acting it), the
adornment of their visual appearance[53] will
perforce constitute some part of the making
of tragedy; and song-composition and verbal
expression also, for those are the media in
which they perform the imitation. By "verbal
expression" I mean the actual composition of
35   the | verses,[54] and by "song-composition"
something whose meaning is entirely clear.[55]

Next, since it is an imitation of an action
and is enacted by certain people who are per-
forming the action, and since those people
must necessarily have certain traits both of
character and thought (for it is thanks to these
38 | 50a1   two factors that we speak of people's | actions
also as having a defined character, and it is in
accordance with their actions that all either
succeed or fail); and since the imitation of the
action is the plot, for by "plot" I mean here
5   the | structuring of the events, and by the
"characters" that in accordance with which
we say that the persons who are acting[56] have
a defined moral character, and by "thought"
all the passages in which they attempt to prove
some thesis or set forth an opinion—it follows
of necessity, then, that tragedy as a whole[57]
has just six constituent elements, in relation to
the essence that makes it a distinct species; and
they are plot, characters, verbal expression, |
10   thought, visual adornment, and song-composi-

tion. For the elements by which they imitate
are two (i.e., verbal expression and song-com-
position), the manner in which they imitate is
one (visual adornment), the things they imitate
are three (plot, characters, thought), and there
is nothing more beyond these. These then are
the constituent forms they use.[58] |

10
The relative importance of the six elements

15   The greatest of these elements is the struc-
turing of the incidents. For tragedy is an imita-
tion not of men but of a life, an action,[59] and
they have moral quality in accordance with
their characters but are happy or unhappy |
20   in accordance with their actions; hence they
are not active in order to imitate their char-
acters, but they include the characters along
with the actions for the sake of the latter. Thus
the structure of events, the plot, is the goal of
tragedy, and the goal is the greatest thing of
all.
        Again: a tragedy cannot exist without a
25   plot, but it can | without characters: thus the
tragedies of most of our modern poets are de-
void of character, and in general many poets
are like that; so also with the relationship be-
tween Zeuxis and Polygnotus, among the
painters: Polygnotus is a good portrayer of
character, while Zeuxis' painting has no dimen-
sion of character at all.
        Again: if one strings end to end speeches

that are expressive of character and carefully
30   worked in thought | and expression, he still
will not achieve the result which we said was
the aim of tragedy; the job will be done much
better by a tragedy that is more deficient in
these other respects but has a plot, a structure
<39 | 50b   of events. <It[60] is much the same case as |
with painting: the most beautiful pigments
smeared on at random will not give as much
pleasure as a black-and-white outline pic-
3>   ture.> Besides, the most powerful means trag-
edy has for swaying our feelings, namely the
35   peripeties and recognitions, | are elements of
plot.

Again: an indicative sign is that those who
are beginning a poetic career manage to hit
the mark in verbal expression and character
portrayal sooner than they do in plot construc-
tion; and the same is true of practically all the
earliest poets.

So plot is the basic principle, the heart
and soul, as it were, of tragedy, and the char-
(39...b3)   acters come second: (. . .) it is the imitation
of an action and imitates the persons primarily
for the sake of their action.

5   Third in rank is thought. This | is the
ability[61] to state the issues and appropriate
points pertaining to a given topic, an ability
which[62] springs from the arts of politics and
rhetoric; in fact the earlier poets made their
characters talk "politically," the present-day
poets rhetorically.[63] But "character" is that
kind of utterance which clearly reveals the

bent of a man's moral choice[64] (hence there is
10 no character in that class of utterances | in
which there is nothing at all that the speaker
is choosing or rejecting),[65] while "thought"
is the passages in which they try to prove that
something is so or not so, or state some general
principle.

Fourth is the verbal expression of the
speeches.[66] I mean by this the same thing that
was said earlier, that the "verbal expression"
is the conveyance of thought through lan-
guage: a statement which has the same mean-
15 ing whether one says "verses" or | "speeches."

The song-composition of the remaining
parts is the greatest of the sensuous attrac-
tions,[67] and the visual adornment of the drama-
tic persons can have a strong emotional effect
but is the least artistic element, the least con-
nected with the poetic art; in fact the force
of tragedy can be felt even without benefit
of public performance and actors, while for
20 the production | of the visual effect the prop-
erty man's art is even more decisive than that
of the poets.

11 [7]
General principles of the tragic plot

With these distinctions out of the way,
let us next discuss what the structuring of
the events should be like, since this is both the
basic and the most important element in the
tragic art. We have established, then, that trag-

edy is an imitation of an action which is com-
25 plete | and whole and has some magnitude
(for there is also such a thing as a whole that
has no magnitude). "Whole" is that which
has beginning, middle, and end. "Beginning"
is that which does not necessarily follow on
something else, but after it something else
naturally is or happens; "end," the other way
round, is that which naturally follows on some-
30 thing else, either | necessarily or for the most
part, but nothing else after it; and "middle"
that which naturally follows on something else
and something else on it. So, then, well-con-
structed plots should neither begin nor end
at any chance point but follow the guidelines
just laid down.

   Furthermore, since the beautiful, whether
35 a living creature or anything | that is composed
of parts,[68] should not only have these in a
fixed order to one another but also possess a
definite size which does not depend on chance
—for beauty depends on size and order; hence
neither can a very tiny creature turn out to
be beautiful (since our perception of it grows
blurred as it approaches the period of imper-
ceptibility) nor an excessively huge one (for
39 | 51a1 then it cannot all | be perceived at once and
so its unity and wholeness are lost), if for ex-
ample there were a creature a thousand miles
long—so, just as in the case of living creatures
they must have some size, but one that can
5 be taken in in a single view, so | with plots:
they should have length, but such that they

are easy to remember. As to a limit of the
length, the one is determined by the tragic
competitions and the ordinary span of atten-
tion.[69] (If they had to compete with a hundred
tragedies they would compete by the water
clock, as they say used to be done [?].)[70]
10 But the limit fixed by the very nature | of the
case is: the longer the plot, up to the point of
still being perspicuous as a whole, the finer
it is so far as size is concerned; or to put it in
general terms, the length in which, with things
happening in unbroken sequence, a shift takes
place either probably or necessarily from bad
to good fortune or from good to bad—that
15 is an acceptable | norm of length.[71]

[8]

But a plot is not unified, as some people
think, simply because it has to do with a single
person. A large, indeed an indefinite number
of things can happen to a given individual,
some of which go to constitute no unified
event; and in the same way there can be many
acts of a given individual from which no single
action emerges. Hence it seems clear that those
20 poets | are wrong who have composed *Hera-
cleïds*, *Theseïds*, and the like. They think that
since Heracles was a single person it follows
that the plot will be single too. But Homer,
superior as he is in all other respects, appears
to have grasped this point well also, thanks
25 either to art or nature, for in composing | an
Odyssey he did not incorporate into it every-
thing that happened to the hero, for example

how he was wounded on Mt. Parnassus[72] or
how he feigned madness at the muster, neither
of which events, by happening, made it at all
necessary or probable that the other should
happen. Instead, he composed the *Odyssey*—
and the *Iliad* similarly—around a unified ac-
tion of the kind we have been talking about. |

30   A poetic imitation, then, ought to be uni-
fied in the same way as a single imitation in
any other mimetic field, by having a single
object: since the plot is an imitation of an
action, the latter ought to be both unified and
complete, and the component events ought
to be so firmly compacted that if any one of
them is shifted to another place, or removed,
the whole is loosened up and dislocated; for
35   an element whose addition | or subtraction
makes no perceptible extra difference is not
really a part of the whole.

[9]

From what has been said it is also clear
that the poet's job is not to report what has
happened but what is likely to happen: that
is, what is capable of happening according to
38 | the rule of probability or necessity. Thus |
51b1   the difference between the historian and the
poet is not in their utterances being in verse
or prose (it would be quite possible for Hero-
dotus' work to be translated into verse, and
it would not be any the less a history with
verse than it is without it); the difference
lies in the fact that the historian speaks of |
5   what has happened, the poet of the kind of

thing that *can* happen. Hence also poetry is
a more philosophical and serious business than
history; for poetry speaks more of universals,
history of particulars. "Universal" in this case
is what kind of person is likely to do or say cer-
tain kinds of things, according to probability
10 or necessity; that is what | poetry aims at, al-
though it gives its persons particular names
afterward; while the "particular" is what Al-
cibiades did or what happened to him.[73]

In the field of comedy this point has been
grasped: our comic poets construct their plots
on the basis of general probabilities and then
assign names to the persons quite arbitrarily,
instead of dealing with individuals as the old
15 iambic poets | did. But in tragedy they still
cling to the historically given names.[74] The
reason is that what is possible is persuasive; so
what has not happened we are not yet ready to
believe is possible, while what has happened
is, we feel,[75] obviously possible: for it would
not have happened if it were impossible.
Nevertheless, it is a fact that even in our trag-
20 edies, in some cases only one | or two of the
names are traditional, the rest being invented,
and in some others none at all. It is so, for ex-
ample, in Agathon's *Antheus*—the names in
it are as fictional as the events—and it gives no
less pleasure because of that. Hence the poets
ought not to cling at all costs to the traditional
25 plots, around which our tragedies are | con-
structed. And in fact it is absurd to go search-
ing for this kind of authentication, since even

the familiar names are familiar to only a few
in the audience and yet give the same kind of
pleasure to all.

So from these considerations it is evident
that the poet should be a maker[76] of his plots
more than of his verses, insofar as he is a poet
by virtue of his imitations and what he imitates
is actions. Hence even if it happens that he
puts something that has actually taken place
30   into poetry, | he is none the less a poet; for
there is nothing to prevent some of the things
that have happened from being the kind of
things that can happen, and that is the sense in
which he is their maker.

12
Simple and complex plots

Among simple plots and actions[77] the epi-
sodic are the worst. By "episodic" plot I mean
one in which there is no probability or neces-
35   sity for the order in which the | episodes fol-
low one another. Such structures are composed
by the bad poets because they are bad poets,
but by the good poets because of the actors:
in composing contest pieces for them, and
38 | stretching out the plot beyond its capacity,[78] |
52a1   they are forced frequently to dislocate the se-
quence.

Furthermore, since the tragic imitation is
not only of a complete action but also of events
that are fearful and pathetic, and these come
about best when they come about contrary to
one's expectation yet logically, one following

from the other; that way they will be more
5 productive | of wonder than if they happen
merely at random, by chance—because even
among chance occurrences the ones people
consider most marvelous are those that seem
to have come about as if on purpose: for ex-
ample the way the statue of Mitys at Argos
killed the man who had been the cause of
Mitys' death, by falling on him while he was
attending the festival; it stands to reason, peo-
10 ple think, that such things | don't happen by
chance—so plots of that sort cannot fail to be
artistically superior.

[10]

Some plots are simple, others are com-
plex;[79] indeed the actions of which the plots
are imitations already fall into these two cate-
gories. By "simple" action I mean one the de-
15 velopment of which | being continuous and
unified in the manner stated above,[80] the re-
versal comes without peripety or recognition,
and by "complex" action one in which the
reversal is continuous but with recognition or
peripety or both. And these developments must
grow out of the very structure of the plot it-
self, in such a way that on the basis of what
has happened previously this particular out-
20 come follows | either by necessity or in ac-
cordance with probability; for there is a great
difference in whether these events happen be-
cause of those or merely after them.

[11]

"Peripety" is a shift of what is being
undertaken to the opposite in the way previ-

ously stated,[81] and that in accordance with
probability or necessity as we have just been
25   saying; as for example in the *Oedipus* | the
man who has come, thinking that he will re-
assure Oedipus, that is, relieve him of his fear
with respect to his mother, by revealing who
he once was, brings about the opposite; and
in the *Lynceus*,[82] as he (Lynceus) is being led
away with every prospect of being executed,
and Danaus pursuing him with every prospect
of doing the executing, it comes about as a
result of the other things that have happened
in the play that *he* is executed and Lynceus
30   is saved. And "recognition" is, | as indeed the
name indicates, a shift from ignorance to
awareness, pointing in the direction either of
close blood ties or of hostility, of people who
have previously been in a clearly marked state
of happiness or unhappiness.

The finest recognition is one that happens
at the same time as a peripety, as is the case
with the one in the *Oedipus*. Naturally, there
are also other kinds of recognition: it is pos-
sible for one to take place in the prescribed
35   manner in relation to | inanimate objects and
chance occurrences, and it is possible to recog-
nize whether a person has acted or not acted.
But the form that is most integrally a part of
the plot, the action, is the one aforesaid; for
that kind of recognition combined with peri-
38 | 52b1   pety will excite either pity | or fear (and these
are the kinds of action of which tragedy is an
imitation according to our definition),[83] be-

cause both good and bad fortune will also be most likely to follow that kind of event. Since, further, the recognition is a recognition of persons, some are of one person by the other

5 one only (when it is already known who | the "other one" is), but sometimes it is necessary for both persons to go through a recognition, as for example Iphigenia is recognized by her brother through the sending of the letter, but of him by Iphigenia another recognition is required.

These then are two elements of plot:

10 peripety | and recognition; third is the *pathos*. Of these, peripety and recognition have been discussed; a *pathos* is a destructive or painful act, such as deaths on stage, paroxysms of pain, woundings, and all that sort of thing.[84]

13 [12]
The tragic side of tragedy: pity and fear and the patterns of the complex plot

The "parts" of tragedy which should be used as constituent elements were mentioned

[13]

(15-28) earlier;[85] (. . .) but what one should aim at and what one should avoid in composing one's

30 plots, and whence the effect of tragedy is | to come, remains to be discussed now, following immediately upon what has just been said.

Since, then, the construction of the finest tragedy should be not simple but complex,[86] and at the same time imitative of fearful and

pitiable happenings (that being the special
character of this kind of poetry), it is clear
first of all that (1)[87] neither should virtuous
men appear undergoing | a change from good
to bad fortune, for that is not fearful, nor
pitiable either, but morally repugnant; nor (2)
the wicked from bad fortune to good—that
is the most untragic form of all, it has none of
the qualities that one wants: it is productive
neither of ordinary sympathy[88] | nor of pity
nor of fear—nor again (3) the really wicked
man changing from good fortune to bad, for
that kind of structure will excite sympathy
but neither pity nor fear, since the one (pity)
is directed towards the man who does not de-
serve his misfortune and the other | (fear)
towards the one who is like the rest of man-
kind[89]—what is left is the man who falls be-
tween these extremes. Such is a man who is
neither a paragon of virtue and justice nor
undergoes the change to misfortune through
any real badness or wickedness but because
of | some mistake; one of those who stand in
great repute and prosperity, like Oedipus and
Thyestes: conspicuous men from families of
that kind.

So, then, the artistically made plot must
necessarily be single rather than double, as
some maintain, and involve a change not from
bad fortune to good fortune but the other way
round, | from good fortune to bad, and not
thanks to wickedness but because of some mis-
take of great weight and consequence, by a

35

38 | 53a1

5

10

15

man such as we have described or else on the good rather than the bad side. An indication comes from what has been happening in tragedy: at the beginning the poets used to "tick off" whatever plots came their way, but nowadays the finest tragedies are composed about
20 a few houses: | they deal with Alcmeon, Oedipus, Orestes, Meleager, Thyestes, Telephus, and whichever others have had the misfortune to do or undergo fearful things.

Thus the technically finest tragedy is based on this structure. Hence those who bring
25 charges against Euripides for doing | this in his tragedies[90] are making the same mistake.[91] His practice is correct in the way that has been shown. There is a very significant indication: on our stages and in the competitions, plays of this structure are accepted as[92] the most tragic, *if* they are handled successfully, and Euripides, though he may not make his other arrangements effectively, still is felt by
30 the audience to be | the most tragic, at least, of the poets.

Second comes the kind which is rated first by certain people, having its structure double like the *Odyssey* and with opposite endings for the good and bad. Its being put first is due to the weakness of the audiences;
35 for the poets follow along, catering | to their wishes. But this particular pleasure is not the one that springs from tragedy but is more characteristic of comedy.[93]

14 [14]
Pity and fear and the tragic act[94]

| 53b1 | Now it is possible for the fearful or
pathetic effect to come from the actors' ap-
pearance,[95] but it is also possible for it to arise
from the very structure of the events, and this
is closer to the mark and characteristic of a
better poet. Namely, the plot must be so struc-
tured, even without benefit of any visual ef-
5   fect, that the one | who is hearing the events
unroll shudders with fear and feels pity at what
happens: which is what one would experience
on hearing the plot of the *Oedipus*.[96] To set
out to achieve this by means of the masks and
costumes is less artistic, and requires technical
support in the staging. As for those who do
not set out to achieve the fearful through the
10   masks and costumes, | but only the monstrous,
they have nothing to do with tragedy at all;
for one should not seek any and every pleasure
from tragedy, but the one that is appropriate
to it.

Since it is the pleasure derived from pity
and fear by means of imitation that the poet
should seek to produce, it is clear that these
qualities must be built into the constituent
events. Let us determine, then, which kinds of
15   happening are felt by the spectator | to be
fearful, and which pitiable. Now such acts are
necessarily the work of persons who are near
and dear (close blood kin) to one another, or
enemies, or neither. But when an enemy at-

tacks an enemy there is nothing pathetic about
either the intention or the deed, except in the
actual pain suffered by the victim; nor when
the act is done by "neutrals"; but when the
tragic acts come within the limits of close |
20 blood relationship, as when brother kills or in-
tends to kill brother or do something else of
that kind to him, or son to father or mother
to son or son to mother—those are the situa-
tions one should look for.[97]

Now although it is not admissible to break
up the transmitted stories—I mean for instance
that Clytemestra was killed by Orestes, or
25 Eriphyle by | Alcmeon—one should be artis-
tic both in inventing stories and in managing
the ones that have been handed down. But
what we mean by "artistic"[98] requires some
explanation.

It is possible, then, (1) for the act to be
performed as the older poets presented it,
knowingly and wittingly; Euripides did it that
way also, in Medea's murder of her children.
It is possible (2) to refrain from performing
the deed, with knowledge.[99] Or it is possible |
30 (3) to perform the fearful act, but unwit-
tingly, then recognize the blood relationship
later, as Sophocles' Oedipus does; in that case
the act is outside the play, but it can be in the
tragedy itself, as with Astydamas' Alcmeon,
or Telegonus in the *Wounding of Odysseus*.
A further mode,[100] in addition to these, is (4)
35 while | intending because of ignorance to per-
form some black crime, to discover the rela-

tionship before one does it. And there is no
other mode besides these; for one must neces-
sarily either do the deed or not, and with or
without knowledge of what it is.

Of these modes, to know what one is do-
ing but hold off and not perform the act (no.
2) is worst: it has the morally repulsive char-
acter[101] and at the same time is not tragic; for

39 | 54a1   there is no tragic act. Hence nobody | com-
poses that way, or only rarely, as, for example,
Haemon threatens Creon in the *Antigone*. Per-
forming the act (with knowledge) (no. 1) is
second (poorest). Better is to perform it in
ignorance and recognize what one has done
afterward (no. 3); for the repulsive quality
does not attach to the act, and the recognition
has a shattering emotional effect. But the best

5 | is the last (no. 4): I mean a case like the one
in the *Cresphontes* where Merope is about to
kill her son but does not do so because she
recognizes him first;[102] or in *Iphigenia in Tauris*
the same happens with sister and brother; or
in the *Helle* the son recognizes his mother just
as he is about to hand her over to the enemy.

The reason[103] for what was mentioned a
while ago, namely that our tragedies have to

10   do | with only a few families, is this: It was
because the poets, when they discovered how
to produce this kind of effect in their plots,
were conducting their search on the basis of
chance, not art; hence they have been forced
to focus upon those families which happen to
have suffered tragic happenings of this kind.

15
The tragic characters

Enough, then, concerning the structure
15 of events and what traits the | tragic plots
[15]
should have. As for the characters, there are
four things to be aimed at. First and foremost,
that they be good. The persons will have char-
acter if in the way previously stated[104] their
speech or their action reveals the moral quality
20 of some choice, and good character if | a good
choice. Good character exists, moreover, in
each category of persons: a woman can be
good, or a slave, although one of these classes
(*sc.* women) is inferior and the other, as a
class, worthless. Second, that they be appro-
priate; for it is possible for a character to be
brave, but inappropriately to a woman.[105]
Third is likeness to human nature in general;
25 for this is different | from making the character
good and appropriate according to the criteria
previously mentioned. And fourth is consis-
tency. For even if the person being imitated is
inconsistent, and that kind of character has
been taken as the theme, he should be incon-
sistent in a consistent fashion.

An example of moral depravity that ac-
complishes no necessary purpose is the Mene-
30 laus in Euripides' *Orestes;* of an | unsuitable
and inappropriate character, the lamentation
of Odysseus in the *Scylla* and the speech of
Melanippe;[106] and of the inconsistent, Iphi-

genia at Aulis; for the girl who pleads for her life is in no way like the later one.[107]

In character portrayal also, as in plot construction, one should always strive for either the necessary or the probable, | so that it is either necessary or probable for that kind of person to do or say that kind of thing, just as it is for one event to follow the other. It is evident, then, that the dénouements of plots also should come out of the character | itself,[108] and not from the "machine"[109] as in the *Medea* or with the sailing of the fleet in the *Aulis*.[110] Rather the machine should be used for things that lie outside the drama proper, either previous events that a human being cannot know, or subsequent events which | require advance prophecy and exposition; for we grant the gods the ability to foresee everything. But let there be no illogicality in the web of events, or if there is, let it be outside the play like the one in Sophocles' *Oedipus*.

Since tragedy is an imitation of persons who are better than average, one should imitate the good portrait | painters, for in fact, while rendering likenesses of their sitters by reproducing their individual appearance, they also make them better-looking; so the poet, in imitating men who are irascible or easygoing or have other traits of that kind, should make them, while still plausibly drawn, morally good,[111] as Homer portrayed Achilles as good yet like other men. |

16 [16]
[*Techniques of recognition*[112]

What recognition is generically, was stated earlier;[113] now as to its varieties: First |
20 comes the one that is least artistic and is most used, merely out of lack of imagination, that by means of tokens. Of these some are inherited, like "the lance that all the Earth-born wear,"[114] or "stars" such as Carcinus employs in his *Thyestes;* some are acquired, and of those some are on the body, such as scars, others are external, like the well-known amu-
25 lets or the recognition | in the *Tyro* by means of the little ark. There are better and poorer ways of using these; for example, Odysseus was recognized in different ways by means of his scar, once by the nurse and again by the swineherds. Those that are deliberately cited for the sake of establishing an identity, and all that kind, are less artistic, while those that develop naturally but unexpectedly, like the one
30 in the foot-washing scene,[115] | are better.

Second poorest are those that are contrived by the poet and hence are inartistic; for example the way, in the *Iphigenia,* she recognizes that it is Orestes: *she* was recognized by means of the letter, but *he* goes out of his way to say what the poet, rather than the plot, wants him to say. Thus this mode is close kin |
35 to the error mentioned above:[116] he might as well have actually worn some tokens. Simi-

larly, in Sophocles' *Tereus*, the "voice of the shuttle."[117]

Third poorest is that through recollection, by means of a certain awareness that follows on seeing or hearing something, like the one in *38 | 55a1* the *Cypriotes* | of Dicaeogenes where the hero bursts into tears on seeing the picture, and the one in Book 8 of the *Odyssey:* Odysseus weeps when he hears the lyre-player and is reminded of the War; in both cases the recognition follows.

Fourth in ascending order is the recognition based on reasoning; for example in the *Libation-Bearers:* "Somebody like me has 5 come; nobody is | like me but Orestes; therefore he has come." And the one suggested by the sophist Polyidus in speaking of the *Iphigenia:* it would have been natural, he said, for Orestes to draw the conclusion (aloud): "My sister was executed as a sacrifice, and now it is my turn." Also in the *Tydeus* of Theodectes: "I came expecting to find my son, and instead I am being destroyed myself." Or the one in 10 the *Daughters of Phineus:* | when they see the spot they reflect that it was indeed their fate to die here; for they had been exposed here as babies also. There is also one based on mistaken inference on the part of the audience, as in *Odysseus the False Messenger*. In that play, that he and no one else can string the bow is an assumption, a premise invented by the poet, and also his saying that he would recognize the bow when in fact he had not seen it;

whereas the notion that he (the poet) had
made his invention for the sake of the other
person who would make the recognition, |
15   that is a mistaken inference.[118]

The best recognition of all is the one that
arises from the events themselves; the emo-
tional shock of surprise is then based on prob-
abilities, as in Sophocles' *Oedipus* and in the
Iphigenia; for it was only natural that she
should wish to send a letter. Such recognitions
are the only ones that dispense with artificial
20   inventions | and visible tokens. And second-
best are those based on reasoning.]

17
Essential procedures in converting
a plot into a play[119]

[15]
Watch these points, then, and also the
perceptions that necessarily attend on the po-
etic art.[120] We have spoken about them in our
[17]
published discourses; anyhow, in constructing
one's plots and working them out in language
one should put them directly before one's
eyes as much as possible. That way, seeing
most vividly, as if he were actually getting
25   close to the events | as they happen, the poet
can devise the appropriate "business," and dis-
crepancies are least likely to escape his notice.
A case in point is the criticism that was di-
rected at Carcinus: Amphiaraus was discov-

ered coming back from the sanctuary, a
circumstance which the poet failed to notice
because he was not visualizing the action, but
on the stage the play failed because the spec-
tators were offended by it. Also one should
30 work the appropriate figures | and forms of
speech[121] into the text, as far as possible. For
people in the grip of the passions are most
persuasive because they share the same natural
tendencies we have, and it is the man who con-
veys dejection or rages with anger in the most
natural terms who makes us feel dejection or
anger.

(Hence the composition of poetry is an
affair of either the well-endowed or[122] the
manic individual; for of these two types the
ones are impressionable while the others are
liable to be "possessed" from time to time.)

And the argument of the play, whether
34 | previously made or | in process of composition
55b1 by oneself, should first be sketched out in ab-
stract form and only then expanded and other
scenes ("episodes") added.[123] I mean, as a
method for gaining a general view of the play,
the following, for example with the *Iphigenia:*
A certain young woman is sacrificed but spir-
ited away without the sacrificers perceiving
it. She is established in another country, where
5 | the custom is to sacrifice all foreigners to
their goddess, and wins this priesthood. A con-
siderable while later the priestess's brother
happens to come to the country (the fact that
the god ordered him to do so, and for what

purpose, is outside of the plot),[124] and having
come and been captured he is about to be sacri-
(9–11)   ficed when he recognizes his sister,[125] | (. . .)
and thence comes his deliverance. At this stage,
but not before, one may assign names to the
characters and add other scenes; but be sure
that these are appropriate, as for example the
fit of madness through which he is captured
and their escape by means of the purification
15   ceremony | are appropriate to[126] Orestes.

But in dramas the episodes are short,
whereas the epic gets its length from them.
Thus the actual argument of the *Odyssey* is
not long: A certain man has been away from
home for many years, being kept from return-
ing by a god,[127] and is alone. Further, things
20   at home are in such a state that his | property
is being eaten up by suitors and an ambush is
laid against his son. He himself arrives home
after a series of hardships, and having recog-
nized certain people mounts his attack, him-
self survives, and destroys his enemies. This
is the core of the poem; the rest is episodes.

18 [18]
"Tying" and "untying" of the plot; the marvelous; the chorus

One part of every tragedy is the tying, the
25   other is the untying:[128] | the events that lie
outside the play, and in many cases some of
those inside, are the tying, the rest is the un-
tying. By "tying" I mean the part from the

beginning through the last scene preceding the shift to good or bad fortune, and by "untying" the part from the beginning of the shift to the end. Thus in the *Lynceus* of Theodectes |

30 the tying includes the events that have taken place before the play begins, the capture of the child, and, again, of the couple,[129] and the untying includes everything from the indictment for murder to the end.

There are four kinds of tragedy (that being also the number of the "parts" that have been mentioned):[130] the complex, which is all

34 | peripety and recognition; the fatal, like | the

56a1 Ajax and Ixion plays; the moral, such as the *Women of Phthia* and the *Peleus;* and the episodic,[131] like *Daughters of Phorcys, Prometheus,* and all the Hades dramas.[132]

One must try if possible to have all these features, or if not, the biggest ones and as many of them as one can manage. This is especially

5 so | when one considers how unfairly they criticize the dramatists nowadays. We have had poets who were good in this or that particular line, but they now expect every individual to surpass each of them in his own specialty; whereas the fair thing is to assess tragedies as different or the same by virtue of nothing so much as their plot: that is, those dramas that have the same tying and untying (are the

10 same). Many poets tie their plots well | but untie them poorly, but the two must be smoothly adjusted to one another.

One should also remember what has been

said here repeatedly,[133] and not make an epic
mass of incidents into a tragedy (by "epic" I
mean that which includes many stories): as
would be the case, for example, if one should
dramatize the story of the *Iliad* whole.[134] In
the epic, thanks to its length, the sections take
15 on a fitting size, but | in dramas the outcome
is very different from what one intended. An
indication: the poets who have dramatized
the Sack of Troy whole, instead of part-wise
as Euripides did with Hecuba[135] (not as Aes-
chylus did), either do not place in the competi-
tion at all or fail to win. Thus that was the
only competition in which Agathon failed to
20 place. In both peripeties and | simple actions,
on the other hand, they achieve the marvelous
effects they are aiming at.[136] And that happens
when the fellow who is clever but has a streak
of villainy in him is fooled, like Sisyphus, or
the one who is brave but unjust to others is
defeated. And this result is even logical, in the
sense of Agathon's remark: namely, it is logical
25 that many things should happen | which are
illogical.

The chorus also should be thought of as
one of the actors;[137] it should be a part of the
whole and contribute its share to success in
the competitive effort in the manner of Sopho-
cles, not Euripides. For the pieces that are sung
during the plays of other poets no more be-
long to the particular plot than they do to
some other. Hence it is a common practice
now to sing "inserted lyrics" (Agathon first |

30 began doing so); and yet what difference is there between singing inserted lyrics and inserting a speech from one play into another—or a whole scene?

19 [19]
Thought

The other elements have now been discussed, and it remains to speak of verbal expression and thought. For a discussion of
35 "thought," then, please consult | our treatise on rhetoric, for the problem is particularly connected with that discipline.

Under "thought" fall all the effects that have to be deliberately and consciously achieved through the use of speech. Elements of this endeavor are (1) proof and refutation
38 | and (2) the stimulation of feelings such as |
56b1 pity, fear,[138] anger, and the like.[139] Now it is evident that one must use the same practices in tragic actions as in everyday life, when it is a question of making things appear pitiable or fearful, or important or probable. There
5 is just this much | difference, that the emotional effects ought to carry across to the spectator without explicit argument, while the proofs have to be deliberately produced in speech, by the speaker, and come as a result of the speech. For what would be the use of a speaker if things appeared in the wished-for light without the speech?

20
Verbal expression; the elements of language

Among the phenomena of expression through language, one branch of theory has to do with the modes of utterance; for example, what is a command and what a prayer; statement and threat, question and answer, and so on. Knowledge of these belongs to the art

10 of delivery | and concerns the man who possesses the master-art of poetic interpretation. But not the poet; for no criticism worth serious attention is directed towards poetry on the basis of knowledge or ignorance of these matters. Who, for example, would agree with

15 | Protagoras' carping criticism of Homer, that the poet has committed an error by uttering a command when he thinks he is making a prayer: "Sing, goddess, the wrath" (to order someone to do something or not is a command, says Protagoras)? So we will ignore this kind of question on the ground that it has nothing to do with poetry.

[20]

20 Speech as a whole[140] has | eight parts: letter, syllable, conjunction, noun, verb, article, inflection, utterance.

1. A letter,[141] then, is an indivisible sound, not any and every one however, but one from which a composite sound naturally arises. (Animals utter indivisible sounds too, but I do not call any of them a letter.) Its subdivisions

25 are | vowel, half-vowel, and mute. "Vowel"

is a letter that has an audible sound without
the addition of another letter; "half-vowel,"
one that has an audible sound *with* the addi-
tion of another letter—for example, *s* and *r;*
"mute," a letter that has no sound by itself
when a letter is added, but becomes audible
30 when combined with one of those | that have
a sound—for example, *g* and *d.* The letters
differ according to the configuration of the
mouth, the place of utterance, aspiration and
non-aspiration, length and shortness, also by
virtue of acute, grave, and intermediate pitch.
To investigate these things in detail is the job
of the metrician.[142]

2. A syllable is a non-meaningful compos-
35 ite sound | made up of a mute and a vowel or
half-vowel: for example, *gr* (is a syllable?)
either with (*gra*) or without *a* (*gr*). But these
differentiations also are the business of metrics.

3. A conjunction[143] is either:

(a) a non-meaningful sound which
38 | 57a1 neither prevents nor produces a single | mean-
ingful sound which is capable of being formed
out of several sounds, and which it is not
proper to put at the beginning of an utterance,
by itself—for example, *men, êtoi, de*; or

(b) a non-meaningful sound which is
naturally capable of making a single meaning-
5 ful sound | out of two or more meaningful
sounds—for example, *amphi, peri,* and the
like.

4. An article is a non-meaningful sound
which marks the beginning or end or transi-

tion point of an utterance, being naturally
10 suitable to put at either end | or in the middle.

5. A noun[144] is a meaningful composite
sound without tense, no part of which is mean-
ingful by itself; for in two-part compounds we
do not use the part as having meaning in and
by itself; thus in *Theodoros* (lit. 'god's gift')
the *-doros* ('gift') does not carry meaning.

6. A verb is a meaningful composite sound
15 with tense, no part of which is meaningful |
by itself, as was the case with nouns: thus
"man" or "white" does not convey any tense
meaning, but "is walking," "has walked" sig-
nifies in the one case present, in the other case
past time.

7. Inflection[145] applies to nouns and verbs
and signifies either the "of" or "to" relationship
20 and all that, | or number: for example, "men,"
"man," or in relationship to the modes of ut-
terance, as in question or command; for "Did
he walk?" (*ebadisen;*) and "Walk!" (*badize!*)
are examples of inflection in this sense.

8. An utterance is a composite meaningful
sound, some parts of which mean something
by themselves. Not every utterance is com-
25 posed of nouns | and verbs: for example the
definition of man; thus an utterance may exist
without a verb, but it will always have some
part that means something. An example is
"Cleon" in "Cleon is walking." An utterance
is single in either of two ways, either as signi-
fying one thing—the definition of man— |
30 or by conjunction of several items—the *Iliad*.

21 [21]
Nouns; poetic language, especially metaphor[146]

The classes of nouns:

1. Simple. By "simple" I mean one that is composed of non-meaningful parts: for example, *gê* ('earth').

2. Double. One variety is made up of meaningful and non-meaningful parts (but not so distinguished in the noun itself), the other of meaningful ones. One can also have a triple or quadruple compound noun, even a multiple compound; so with a great many words | in the dialect of Marseilles: *Hermocaïcoxanthus*,
. . . .

Every noun | is either:

1. the regular word for a thing (*kyrion*),
2. a foreign word (*glôtta*, 'gloss'),
3. a metaphor, or
4. an ornamental (*kosmos*),
5. invented (*pepoiêmenon*),
6. lengthened (*ektetamenon*),
7. curtailed (*hyphêirêmenon*), or
8. altered (*exêllagmenon*) word.

I mean by:

(1) "regular word" the one that is employed by a given people; by

(2) "foreign word" one that is employed by other people. Obviously, then, it is possible for the same word | to be both regular and foreign, but not for the same people. Thus *sigynos* (a kind of spear) is a regular word in Cyprus, a foreign word in Athens.

3. Metaphor is the application of the name
of a thing to something else, working either
(a) from genus to species, or (b) from species
to genus, or (c) from species to species, or (d)
by proportion.

a. I mean by "from genus to species" an
10 expression like "my ship | stands here"; for
lying at anchor is one kind of standing.

b. From species to genus: "Verily, ten
thousand good things hath Odysseus wrought":
"ten thousand" is a large number, so it is used
here in place of "many."

c. From species to species: for example,
"draining off the life with bronze," and "cut-
ting with the unwearying bronze"; here the
poet has said "draining off" instead of "cut-
15 ting" | and "cutting" instead of "draining off,"
for both verbs mean "take away."

d. Metaphor by proportion occurs when
the second term is related to the first in the
same way as the fourth to the third; then the
poet may use the second in lieu of the fourth,
or vice versa. And sometimes they may add
the point of reference of the word that has
20 been replaced. Thus | the cup stands in the
same relationship to Dionysus as the shield to
Ares; hence the poet may call a cup "Diony-
sus' shield" or a shield "Ares' cup." Or, as old
age is to life, so evening is to day; then he may
call evening the old age of the day, or Empe-
docles' variant on that phrase, and old age the
evening of life or the sunset of life.

25 Some of the items in the proportion | may
have no special name, but they will be used

analogically none the less. Thus to cast seed is to sow, while casting its flame, with reference to the sun, has no particular name; but this action stands in the same relation to sunlight as the sowing to the seed-grain; hence we find the expression "sowing the god-built flame."

30   There is also another way | of using this kind of metaphor: after applying the strange name to it, to negate one of the things that would naturally follow; thus one might call the shield not the "cup of Ares" but a "wineless cup." . . .[147]

5. An invented word is one which does not exist at all in a given people's speech but is coined by the poet. There do seem to be some words of this kind: for example, *ernyges*

35   for 'horns' | and *arêtêr* for 'priest.'

36 | 58a1   6. Lengthened and (7) curtailed: | the one employing a longer vowel than the regular one, or an added syllable, as in *polêos* for *poleôs* or *Pêlêïadeô* for *Pêleidou*; the other when some part of it has been cut out: for example,

5   *krî, dô,* | *ops*.

8. A word is altered when the poet leaves one part of it unchanged but invents another,

(8–17)   as in *dexiteron* ('right') for *dexion*. (. . .)[148]

22 [22]
The basic principles of poetic style

The specific excellence of verbal expression in poetry is to be clear without being

low. The clearest, of course, is that which
uses the regular words for things; but it is
20   low. Examples are | the style of Cleophon and
of Sthenelus. Impressiveness and avoidance of
familiar language is achieved by the use of
alien terms; and by "alien" I mean dialectal
words, metaphor, lengthening of words, in
short anything other than the standard termi-
nology. But if the whole composition is of that
sort, it will be either a riddle or a piece of
25   barbarism: riddle if made up | of metaphors,
barbarism if made up of foreign words. For
the very essence of a riddle is, while talking
about real things, to make impossible combina-
tions of them, such as "I saw one man glue
bronze upon another with fire,"[149] and the
30   like. | And the result of foreign words is bar-
barism.

So, then, poetic expression should have
some mixture of this kind in it; the one in-
gredient, that of foreign words, metaphor,
ornamental words, and all the other varieties,
will ensure that it is not commonplace or low,
and the common element will ensure clarity.
To this combination of clarity and distinction
34 | 58b1   in language the extending, | curtailing, and
altering of words makes no small contribution;
for being different from the regular form and
thus varying the accustomed pattern, it will
produce an effect of distinction, while at the
same time by virtue of its overlapping with
5   normal usage it will promote | clarity. Hence
those who castigate this kind of style and ridi-

cule the poet for using it are wrong in their
criticism: Euclides the elder, for example, who
jeered that it is easy to write poetry if one is
(8-10)   allowed to lengthen vowels at will. (. . .)

Now it is true that an exaggerated and
obvious effort in this direction makes one
ridiculous. But moderation is a common prin-
ciple applying to all the modes of poetic dic-
tion, not merely these particular ones. It would
be easy to achieve the same effect as Euclides
did by making an unsuitable use of metaphors
or foreign words or any of the other cate-
gories, with the deliberate intention of ridi-
15   culing them. | How much a proper use of
them lends distinction to a style can be tested
on epic verses by inserting the ordinary prose
forms. So with foreign words, metaphors, or
any of the other devices one can see that what
we say is true if he will substitute the regular
words. Thus Aeschylus and Euripides com-
20   posed the same iambic line; | the latter changed
just one word, substituting a strange word for
the regular one, and his version has the flavor
of high, the other of low style. (Aeschylus
had written in his *Philoctetes:* "the ulcer that
eats the flesh of my foot," and Euripides sub-
(25-59a4)   stituted "feasts on" for "eats.")[150] (. . .)

It is important to make fitting use of all
the devices we have mentioned, including
5   compounds | and foreign words, but by far
the most important thing is to be good at meta-
phor. This is the only part of the job that
cannot be learned from others; on the con-

trary it is a token of high native gifts, for
making good metaphors depends on perceiving
the likenesses in things.

Of the various kinds of words, compounds
are best suited to the dithyramb, foreign
10 words to epic verse, and metaphors | to iam-
bic verse. (Actually, all the varieties are use-
ful in epic verses, while in iambics, because
they are closest to actual speech, the appro-
priate expressions are those that one might
also use in prose, and they include the regular
names of things, metaphor, and the ornamen-
tal word.)

23
Basic principles of epic composition; Homer

15 Concerning tragedy, then, | that is, the
kind of imitation that works through action,
let us consider that we have now said enough;
[23]
we turn to the kind which is narrative and
works in verse.[151]

It is clear that epic plots should be made
dramatic, as in tragedies, dealing with a single
action which is whole and complete and has
20 beginning, middles, and end, | so that like a
single complete creature[152] it may produce the
appropriate pleasure. It is also clear that the
plot-structure should not resemble a history,
in which of necessity a report is presented not
of a single action but of a single period, in-

cluding everything that happened during that
time to individuals or groups—of which events
each has only chance relationships to the
25   others. For just | as the sea battle at Salamis
and the battle against the Carthaginians in
Sicily took place about the same time of year
but in no way pointed toward the same goal,
so also in successive periods spread over time
it often happens that one event follows another
without any single result coming from them.
Yet, speaking by and large, most poets com-
30   pose | this way.

That is why, in addition to what has
been said about him previously,[153] one can
hardly avoid feeling that Homer showed god-
like genius in this case also, namely in the fact
that although the Trojan War had a begin-
ning and an end, he did not undertake to com-
pose it as a whole[154] either.[155] For the plot
would have been bound to turn out too long
and not easy to encompass in a glance, or, if
it held to some measurable length, to become
entangled with the diversity of its events. |
35   Instead, he has singled out one part of the
whole and used many of the others as epi-
sodes: the Catalogue of Ships, for example,
and other episodes with which he separates[156]
the parts of his composition. The other poets
37 | compose their work around a single person |
59b1   or around a single period, that is, a single ac-
tion with many parts: so, for example, the
author of the *Cypria* and the *Little Iliad*.
Hence from *Iliad* and *Odyssey* one tragedy
each can be made, or two and no more, but

(5-8) many from the *Cypria* and from the *Little* |
Iliad. (. . .)[157]

[24]

Moreover, epic ought to have[158] its spe-
cies identical with tragedy: that is, be either
10 simple or complex and either moral or | fatal;
and the "parts" (i.e., of the plot) the same,[159]
for it needs peripeties and recognitions as well
as tragic acts.[160] Also that the passages con-
taining thought and the verbal expression be
artistically satisfactory. Homer is the first to
employ all these, and he has done it beautifully
(in fact each of his poems has a particular
15 structure: the *Iliad* simple | and fatal, the
Odyssey complex—there being recognitions
in it from beginning to end—and moral); and
in addition he has surpassed all his rivals in
language and thought.

24

Differences between epic and tragedy

But epic differs from tragedy with respect
to (1) the length of the poem and (2) the
verse.

So far as a formula for the length is con-
cerned, the one stated previously[161] will do
very well: that is, it must be possible for the
20 beginning | and the end to be seen together in
one view. This condition would be met if the
poems were shorter than those of the early
poets but approximated the total mass of the
tragedies presented at one sitting.[162] But the
epic has a very strongly marked special ten-

dency towards extra extension of its bulk. This
is because in the case of tragedy it is not possi-
ble to represent many different parts of the
25   action | as of the time they are performed but
only the part on the stage, involving the actors,
while with the epic, because it is narrative in
character, it is possible to carry through many
portions as of the time they are enacted,[163] and
if these are apposite the total bulk and weight
of the poem is augmented by them. So the
epic has this virtue, and that of diversifying,
30 | that is, inserting diverse episodes.[164] (It is
repetitiveness, which so quickly bores the
spectator, that causes tragedies to fail.)

As for the epic verse, it has found its
way to the mark by a process of trial. If some-
one should compose a narrative imitation in any
other verse form, or in several, it would strike
one as incongruous. For the hexameter is the
35   slowest moving and | weightiest of all verses—
that is why it is the most receptive to foreign
words and metaphors—and narrative imitation
also is different from the other kinds. The
iambic trimeter and trochaic tetrameter, on
37 | 60a1   the other hand, | are verses suited to move-
ment, the one to moral action, the other to
dancing. (It would be even more outlandish
if one should mix them,[165] as Chaeremon did.)
Hence nobody has composed a long poem in
any other verse than the hexameter; instead, in
the way we have indicated the very nature of
the genre teaches one to choose the verse that
5   fits | it.

Homer has many other claims to our
praise, but above all because he alone among
poets is not oblivious of what he should com-
pose.[166] Namely, the poet himself should do as
little of the talking as possible; for in those
parts he is not being an imitator. The other
poets are on stage contesting for the prize the
whole time, and their imitations are few and
far between. He, on the other hand, after a
10 few words | of preface, immediately brings
on stage a man, a woman, some character or
other, and not one of them characterless; they
all have distinct characters.

One should indeed try to incorporate the
astonishing in tragedies, but the irrational,
which is the largest single source of astonish-
ment, is more easily achieved in the epic, on
account of one's not actually seeing the per-
son who is performing the act. Thus the cir-
15 cumstances of | the pursuit of Hector would
appear absurd on a stage—the Achaeans stand-
ing there, not joining in the chase, and Achilles
motioning to them to stay back—whereas in
the epic one does not notice it. And the as-
tonishing does give pleasure. An indication of
this is that we all tend to add something to a
story when we repeat it, assuming that that
will be appreciated.

Homer has also been the great teacher of
other poets in the art of telling lies *comme il*
20 *faut*. | This technique is a matter of false
inference. Namely, if a certain thing B is true
or happens when another thing A is true or

happens, then if B obtains people assume that
A also obtains or is happening; but that is a
false inference. Hence if A is false but B neces-
sarily follows if it is true, one should explicitly
state B, because knowing that this is true |
25 our mind makes the false inference that the
antecedent is true also. An example of this is
the one in the foot-washing scene of the
Odyssey.[167]

One should, on the one hand, choose
events that are impossible but plausible in
preference to ones that are possible but im-
plausible; but on the other hand one's plots
should not be made up of irrational incidents.
Best of all is to have no irrationalities, or if
that cannot be managed, to keep them out of
30 the main plot, like | Oedipus' not knowing
how Laius was killed, rather than *in* the play
like the report of the Pythian games in Soph-
ocles' *Electra* or the hero going all the way
from Tegea to Mysia without uttering a word,
in the *Mysians* of Aeschylus.

Hence to claim that one's plot would have
been destroyed if these things had not been
put in is absurd; that kind of plot should not
be constructed in the first place. But if one
does put them in and they are "gotten across"
35 to the listener in more | or less convincing
fashion, even an absurdity can be tolerated.
Thus it would become evident that the irra-
tionalities in the *Odyssey* connected with the
36 | 60b1 putting ashore of Odysseus on Ithaca | were
intolerable, if an inferior poet should deal with

them. As it is, the poet covers over the irrationality, and so sweetens it, by means of the other good things he introduces. One should work especially hard on the verbal expression, however, in the scenes that have neither action, moral quality, nor thought; for when the situation is the other way round a too brilliant
5 style will tend | to cover up both character portrayals and expressions of thought.

25 [25]
[Epic "problems" and their solutions[168]

Concerning epic problems and solutions and the question how many and what kind of categories they spring from, the answer may appear if we go at the question as follows:

Since the poet is an imitator just like a painter or any other image-maker, he must necessarily imitate things one of three possible
10 ways: (1) the way they were | or are, (2) the way they are said or thought to be, or (3) the way they ought to be. Furthermore, these objects are narrated in a language which includes foreign words, metaphors, and many other distortions of normal usage, all of which we give the poets license to employ.

In addition, poetry and politics, or poetry and any other art, do not have the same stand-
15 ards of correctness;[169] and poetry | itself is subject to two kinds of error, essential and accidental. If, namely, it has made a right choice of a subject for imitation but has failed

in the imitation through its incapacity, the fault is its own; but if the initial choice was wrong—for example the horse with both right legs put forward at once,[170] or any error falling under a particular art, such as medicine or

20 | any other art whatever—the blame does not attach to poetry as such. Thus in the discussion of problems the criticisms must be surveyed and solved on the basis of these distinctions.

First, those that involve the art itself. An impossibility has been worked into the poem; in that case an error has been committed, but correctly committed if it achieves the end of the art; and what this end is has already been stated, namely to make the effect of that or

25 another part of the work | more emotionally shattering. Example: the pursuit of Hector. If, however, the end could have been achieved even more, or no less, by actually following the rules of the appropriate art, the error has been incorrectly committed; for, if possible, no error ought to be committed at all.

Next, where *does* the error lie? Does it

30 have to do with | a technical or scientific matter at all, or with some other accidental factor? For the blame is less if the painter didn't know that a female deer has no horns than if he has painted her unrealistically.

Further, if the criticism alleges that the imitation is untrue, perhaps it was done as it ought to be, as Sophocles said that he portrayed people the way they ought to be portrayed, Euripides the way they are: that is how one should solve the problem.

35   Or, if neither of those | approaches is acceptable, defend on the ground that that's the way the usual story goes: about the gods, for example; for perhaps those stories are neither moral nor true but as bad as Xenophanes made them out to be, but anyhow that

37 | is the way they tell them. |

61a1   Some things, perhaps, are no better to say, but that is how they were: "and their spears stood straight on the butt-end" (*Iliad* 10.152); that was the practice at the time, as it still is with the Illyrians.

    In considering whether something has been artistically said or done by somebody, |

5 one must look not merely to what has been done or said, namely whether it is good or bad, but also to the person who did or said it and to whom, when, by what means, or why he did it—for example, so that a greater good may come about or a greater evil may be averted.

    Some problems should be solved by ref-

10 erence to the use of language. | Thus:

    1. A gloss. Perhaps when the poet says *ourêas* (*Iliad* 1.50) he does not mean the mules but the (human) guards; or that Dolon "was indeed ill-favored in looks (shape)" (*Iliad* 10.316) may mean not crooked of body but ugly of face; for the Cretans say "good-looking" when they mean "fair-faced"; or "mix the wine stronger" (*Iliad* 9.202) may

15 mean not "neat," | as if for wine-bibbers, but "quicker."

    2. Some expressions are metaphorical:

e.g., "all gods and men were sleeping all night long" (*Iliad* 10.1, cf. 2.1),[171] when at the same time he says "aye verily as often as he turned his gaze towards the Trojan plain, (he marveled at) the din of flutes and pipes." The solution is that "all" is said here by way of
20   metaphor for "many," "all" being | a species of "much." And "it alone is not washed" in the baths of Ocean (*Iliad* 18.489, = *Odyssey* 5.275): the best-known individual is "alone."

3. By attention to accent, quantity, and the like. Hippias solved the puzzle over "we give him the right to achieve his wish" (*Iliad* 2.15) by reading "give (to give)," and instead of "a part of it is rotted by rain" (*Iliad* 23.327) "a part is *not* rotted by rain."

4. Some by punctuation or spacing out, as in Empedocles (fr. 35, vv. 14–15 Diels): "Suddenly things became mortal, that had learnt before to be immortal, and unmixed, |
25   before mixed."

5. Some by ambiguity: instead of "more (than two-thirds) of the night is past" read *pleô* as "full"; for the word is ambiguous.

6. Some by the custom of the language: thus wine mixed with water is still called "wine," and the phrase "a greave of new-wrought tin" (*Iliad* 21.592) has the same basis. And men who work iron are "bronze-workers" (*chalkeas*); based on the same idiom is the statement that Ganymede is the "wine-
30   pourer" of Zeus, | though the gods don't drink

wine. (This case could also be treated as belonging under metaphor.)

7. When a word is alleged to involve a contradiction, review how many senses it may have in the given sentence. Thus in "by it (or here: *têi*) the ash spear was stayed" (*Iliad* 20.267), consider how many ways the "here" (*tautêi*, = *têi*) can be meant: at this point or 35 this point, according to one's best | conjecture. In other words, operate the other way round from what Glaucon speaks of, that cer- 36 | 61b1 tain people | make an irrational assumption[172] in advance, take a stand on it, and only then do their reasoning: they blame the author as if *he* had said the thing, if it is in contradiction with their opinion.

This is what has happened in the case of Icarius. The problem arises because they think Icarius was a Spartan, in which case it is 5 strange that | Telemachus did not run into him when he went to Sparta. But the fact of the matter may be as the Cephallenians claim: they say that Odysseus married one of their girls and her father's name was Icadius, not Icarius. So the problem gains its air of plausi- bility from an error of fact.

In general, impossibilities should be re- ferred either to the nature of poetic composi- 10 tion, or to what is better, | or to the common opinion. Thus: (1) For poetic purposes a per- suasive impossibility is preferable to something possible but unpersuasive. (2) (If Zeuxis is criticized on the ground that it is impossible

for people)[173] to be the way he painted them, the answer is: yes, but it is better so; the image *ought* to outdo the originals. (3) Refer irrationalities to common opinion ("that's what they say"), or assert the principle that sometimes it is not irrational; for it stands to reason
15   that things should also | happen against reason.

Verbal contradictions should be judged in the same way as they are by formal refutations—is he talking about the same thing, in relationship to the same thing, and in the same sense?—before making it out to be contradictory[174] either to what he himself is saying or to what a reasonable man believes.

On the other hand the condemnation of either illogicality or badness of character is justified when the poet makes use of the illogi-
20   cality, as | Euripides does Aegeus, or the badness, as he does that of Menelaus in the *Orestes*, without necessity.

Thus the critics' objections fall into five categories: (1) impossibilities, (2) illogicalities, (3) things morally harmful, (4) contradictions, and (5) technical errors, and the solutions can be found under the headings
25   mentioned above; | there are twelve of them.]

26 [26]
Final comparison of epic and tragedy

The question can be raised, which is superior, the epic form of imitation or the tragic.[175] For if, as some say, the less vulgar

genre is superior, and the one that is addressed
to a higher type of listener is less vulgar, it
would clearly follow[176] that an art which
imitates anything and everything is vulgar.
Namely (they say) the actors engage in all
kinds of "business" on the assumption that the
public will not catch what is going on un-
30 less | the actor exaggerates, and so they behave
like the third-rate flute-players who twist and
writhe when they are rendering a discus throw
or pull on the chorus leader when playing the
Scylla. So, they conclude, tragedy is that kind
of art: it is like what the older generation of
actors used to think of the later ones (Myn-
35 niscus used | to call Callippides "ape," on the
ground that he exaggerated too much, and
35 | 62a1 there was a similar opinion about | Pindarus
too). So tragedy as a whole stands in the same
relation to epic as these later actors to the
earlier ones. Epic then, according to these
critics, addresses a superior class of listeners,
who have no need of the gestures and pos-
tures, while tragedy is for the groundlings.
So, being vulgar, it must obviously be inferior.
5 To reply: First, | (1) the charge is not
against the art of poetry but the art of acting.
After all, it is also possible to overdo the ges-
tures in a recital of the epic, like Sosistratus,
or in a singing contest as Mnasitheus of Opus
used to do. Second, (2) not all motion is to
be "censored out," any more than all dancing,
but only that of low characters, the kind of
thing that Callippides was criticized for and

10   others are | nowadays: representing a low
class of women, as they say.

Further, (3) tragedy can do its work
without as well as with movement, just as the
epic can. The quality of a play is evident from
reading alone; so, if tragedy is superior in the
other respects that count, this deficiency need
not be reckoned against it.

Furthermore, (4) because[177] it has every-
15   thing the epic has (it can even | employ the
epic verse) and, what is no small item, the
music besides, that source of the vividest of
our pleasures.

Further, (5) it has the dramatic vividness
in reading as well as in actual performance.[178]

Again, (6) by virtue of the fact that the
18 | 62b1   imitation is finished | in shorter space. For the
more concentrated is more pleasurable than
what is diluted with a great deal of time; I
mean, for example, if someone should put
Sophocles' *Oedipus* in as many verses as the
Iliad.

Further, (7) the imitation produced by
the epic poets is less unified (a sign of this:
5   several tragedies come | from one epic imita-
tion), so that if they do produce a unified plot
it either (1), if briefly presented, seems cur-
tailed or, (2), if it follows the length of the
norm, watery; I mean if the poem is put to-
gether out of a number of actions, as the
Iliad[179] has a number of component parts
10   which also | have size in themselves, and yet
it is constructed as well as possible, that is, is as

nearly an imitation of a single action as an epic can be.

If then, tragedy is superior on all these counts and also (8) with respect to its function as an art (for the two arts should produce not any random pleasure but the one we have specified),[180] it is evident that it must be su-
15 perior, since it attains the purpose | better than the epic does.

Well then, concerning tragedy and epic, both in general and their species and component parts, how many there are and how they differ; the causes of artistic excellence and lack of it; and about critical objections and the answers to them, let this much suffice; . . .[181]

(former chapter 12, 52b15-27)

but measured quantitatively, that is, the separate
sections into which it is divided are the following:
prologue, episode, *exodos*, choral part; and of the
latter one part is *parodos* ('entrance'), another is
stasimon—these are common to all plays—while
"stage arias" and *kommoi* are found in some but not
others.

    "Prologue" is a whole section of tragedy that
20 comes before the entrance (*parodos*) | of the chorus;

    "episode," a whole section of tragedy that
comes between whole choral songs;

    exodos, a whole section of tragedy after which
there is no song of the chorus; and, of the choral
part,

    parodos is the first whole utterance of the
chorus;

    stasimon, a song of the chorus without ana-
paests or trochees;

    and *kommos*, a lamentation shared by the
25 chorus and the stage | characters.

    The "parts" of tragedy which should be used
as constituent elements were mentioned earlier, but

measured quantitatively, that is, the separate sections into which it is divided are these.

B

(21, 58a 8-17)

Of nouns themselves, some are masculine, some are feminine, some are intermediate.* Masculine are all those that end in *n, r,* or *s* and its compounds, of which there are two, *psi* (= *ps*) and *xi* (= *x*); feminine are those that end in long vowels, either those that are always long, *eta* (= *ê*) and omega (= *ô*), or, of the variable ones, those ending in *a*. So the terminations of the masculines and feminines turn out even in number (i.e., three each); for *psi* and *xi* are compounds. No noun ends in a mute or a short vowel (*epsilon* or *omicron*); only three in *iota*, namely *meli, kommi, peperi;* and five in *upsilon:* . . .† The intermediates end in these (i.e., *a, i, y*) and *n* and *s*.

* "Intermediate" rather than "neuter" (*oudetera*) because attention is directed to the endings: neuters use some of each (masculine and feminine) and thus stand between the two categories.

†The five nouns are not given in the Greek manuscripts, except that Giorgio Valla (see Introduction, p. 11) wrote them into the margin of his manuscript from somewhere; the original of the Arabic version had them all. They are, in Valla's order, *pôy napy gony dory asty.* But the list is not complete.

78APPENDIX

C

(22, 58b9-10)

E. wrote *Ĕpĭchărēn eīdōn Mărăthōnădĕ bădī-*
zōnta (true quantity of syllables as marked), to be
read as *Ēpĭchărēn eīdōn Mărăthōnădĕ bādīzōntă,*
and *oūk ān g'ĕrămĕnōs tŏn ĕkeīnoū ēllĕbŏron* as
oūk ān g'ērămĕnōs tŏn ĕkeīnoū ēllēbōrŏn.

D

(22, 58b25-59a4)

So if one should alter *nun de m'eôn oligos te kai*
outidanos kai aeikês by substituting the regular
words: *nun de m'eôn mikros te kai asthenikos kai*
aeidês, or *diphron aeikelion katatheis oligên te trap-*
ezan by substituting *diphron aeikelion katatheis mi-*
kran te trapezan; and for *ēïones boöôsin, ēïones*
krazousin.
Further, Ariphrades ridiculed the tragedians
for using expressions that nobody would utter in
conversation, like *dômatôn apo* instead of *apo*
dômatôn, and *sethen* and *egô de nin* and *Achilleôs*
peri instead of *peri Achilleôs,* and all that sort of
thing. All these expressions help produce the dis-
tinguished effect thanks to their *not* being in the
ordinary language; but he was unaware of that fact.

1. Not simply "art of poetry." Throughout Aristotle's theory *poiêtikê*, 'poetic art,' is conceived actively; *poiêsis*, the actual process of composition (see just below), is the activation, the putting to work, of *poiêtikê*. Similarly, in the list of poetic genres in the next paragraph the active side is emphasized. It must also be remembered that these words, including *poiêtês*, 'poet,' are all formed directly from *poiein*, 'make.' The Greek was constantly reminded by his language that the poet is a maker.

2. *Mimêsis*, 'imitation,' also is active in force (it contains the same suffix *-sis*, = '-ing,' as *poiêsis*). The meaning of "imitation" in Aristotle's thought will emerge gradually. At no point does it mean mere copying of miscellaneous details. Yet "presentation" or "representation" tends to suggest too abstract an idea. The root of *mimêsis* is the human instinct of mimicry (sec. 6).

3. Like most of the points where my interpretation of Aristotle differs from the customary, this one is argued and explained in my book *Aristotle's Poetics: The Argument* (pp. 31–33). Briefly, I believe that the division of genres in this section is bilateral, depending on the combination of melody alone (instrumental music), speech

alone (the "nameless" art, including epic poetry, mimes, and dialogues), and finally melody and speech combined (dithyramb, drama), *with rhythm*. Rhythm is present in all; the presence or absence of the other two factors defines the genres.

4. At this point I have omitted as spurious a sentence (actually not a complete one, for it is tailored, if the text can be trusted, to fit into Aristotle's sentence) which says: "and by means of rhythm itself, without melody, the art of the dancers; for these also, through their rhythmically shaped motions, imitate both characters and feelings and actions." It is possible that the word *pathê*, rendered here by "feelings," should be translated instead "experiences." In that case the idea intended would be that of things undergone ("suffered") by the characters whose story is being pantomimed; cf. the *pathos*, the "tragic happening," at the end of sec. 12. But the genuine Aristotle does not recognize either feelings or experiences as objects of imitation *alongside* acts (actions). The tragic *pathos is* an act.

5. By means of two emendations suggested by Lobel, Kassel secures two arts here. It seems to me clear on the contrary that Aristotle means to lump all these media, *including rhythmical prose* (mimes and Socratic dialogues), together in one grand "art," which then can be subdivided into verse-prose, and verse in turn into single- and multiple-verse forms.

6. The Greek word *logoi* here *designates* "speeches" and *means* prose discourses (speeches used "bare" of music). The mimes of Sophron and Xenarchus appear to have been in rhythmical prose—but then all artistic Greek prose was rhythmical.

7. I.e., dialogues: *Sokratikoi logoi*. We think naturally of Plato's, but he did not invent the genre and was far from being the only practitioner of it. Indeed, one theory maintains that Plato took up the writing of Socratic dialogues in order to correct misinterpretations by others.—At the beginning of this sentence I read *oude* instead of *ouden*.

8. The "remote" form "if somebody should" is significant. Iambic trimeters were the regular dialogue verse of both tragedy and comedy, and there were plenty of poems in elegiac couplets, but nobody had yet composed a whole imitative poem, in Aristotle's sense, in trimeters or elegiacs *and nothing else*.—What is meant by "other verses of that kind" is not clear. Possibly certain mixed forms called "epodes" in which, as in the elegiac couplet, verses of different length and/or metrical character alternated with each other. A number of varieties are found in the fragments of Archilochus, but not all from "imitative" poems.

9. Here a long parenthesis intervenes, undoubtedly from Aristotle's own pen but interrupting the main sequence. In a modern book it would be printed as a footnote. The point of the note is that people do employ a generic term, "poet," "poetry," etc., but they apply it simply to all productions in verse, so that it is skewed: it includes nonpoets, i.e., nonimitators, like Empedocles (and also excludes quasi-poets like Plato).

10. Empedocles' two poems, *On Nature* and *Purifications*, had in fact high poetic qualities, of which Aristotle was quite aware, but Empedocles is not an imitator in Aristotle's sense, so he is not a poet: *voilà tout*.

11. By "kinds of verse" Aristotle means those spoken verses which were regularly used stichically (line after line). There were just four of them: dactylic hexameters, elegiac couplets, iambic trimeters, and trochaic tetrameters. (The "epodes" referred to above, if they were indeed referred to there [see n. 8], would hardly count as extra here, since they were already mixtures of iambic and dactylic verses.) To suppose that Aristotle meant to include also the indefinitely large number of "lyric meters," as we call them (he called them "rhythms"), is absurd.

12. The text which I have translated differs from the usual one in two important respects: (1) I take the three clauses "we could not even . . . ," "nor again if somebody . . . ," "and likewise if . . ." as parallel and belonging to a single sentence which has to do with the concept of namelessness. Into the middle of this long sentence an even longer parenthesis has been inserted: "Except people . . . rather than 'poet.' " (2) I have deleted two short phrases at the end (they are italicized in the following translation). Most editors mark no parenthesis and make Aristotle say, immediately after the remark on Homer and Empedocles: "But by the same token (argument), if anybody should make his imitation by mingling all the metres (verses), as Chaeremon composed a *Centaur*, a *'mixed rhapsody'* from all the metres, *he too (he actually?) should be called a poet*" (i.e., like Homer).— There is reason to suppose that the *Centaur* was some kind of closet-drama intended for a reading public. It therefore (probably) dispensed with a chorus but tried to avert monotony by employing the full repertory of stichic verses.

13. It is not entirely clear why Aristotle has substituted "song and verse" for the original "melody and speech," but they are more concrete terms which perhaps suit the present case a little better. In Greek plays songs do alternate with (spoken) verses.

14. We shall see later (sec. 10) that what tragedy really imitates is not the men but their actions.

15. Not simply "good or bad" (cf. the following note). *The spoudaioi* are "serious" men, and many, perhaps most, of them will also be good, but the most important connotation of Aristotle's term is that they are *noble* characters, men of high seriousness: in short, heroes. Conversely, the *phauloi* are not wicked but what used to be called, in our own South, "low-down, no-'count people."

16. With Gudeman, I omit here a clause which tries to paraphrase but vulgarizes and banalizes Aristotle's thought: "for as to their characters all men differ in vice and virtue."

17. Here I supply a main verb ("they imitate") and omit a phrase referring to men who are average, which I think has crowded out the original verb. Aristotle's genuine theory has no room for a third, median class of people who are imitated by poetry.

18. A clause is omitted: "and Dionysius men 'like,' " i.e., like average men.

19. A reference to dancing is omitted here.

20. A clause, "and Cleophon similar ones," is omitted.

21. *Deilos* in classical Greek means "coward."

22. Actually, it is probably just one Cyclops, the celebrated Polyphemus, who was portrayed nobly by Timotheus in a nome and ignobly (satirically) by Philoxenus in a dithyramb.

23. Literally, "at another time 'bringing on' some character." I have substituted this phrase for one which is customarily interpreted as referring to the assumption of a dramatic character *by the poet:* "he can take another personality as Homer does" (Butcher).

24. "Composes": *poieî*, in the substantive sense which the verb has throughout the *Poetics*. Not "as Homer does."

25. Perhaps by a strict reckoning the "persons performing the imitation" ought to be the poets. But Aristotle chooses to speak as if the dramatic poet gets out of the way and leaves the work of imitating (themselves) to the characters of his drama. Cf. sec. 9, 49b34; sec. 10, 50a20.

26. It is helpful to recognize that this is a separate section, only superficially connected with what precedes and follows and written from a different point of view. It might be a later insertion (in that case, from a period not long after Aristotle) or one by Aristotle himself. The notes on the Dorian claim to the invention of tragedy and comedy betray (contrary to what is often said) sympathy with the Dorian cause.

27. This is not quite accurate if taken literally, since all poets, not merely dramatic poets, imitate men acting (sec. 3 *init.*); but it is clear enough what is meant.

28. At this point I omit a passage which says: "For Epicharmus the poet was from there, being considerably earlier than Chionides and Magnes" (the earliest recorded comic poets at Athens). But Aristotle very likely had Epicharmus in mind.

29. Aristotle does not here identify "those in the Peloponnese," but from other evidence, including a quotation from the lost dialogue *On Poets*, we know almost certainly that he meant Sicyon, and with fair probability that he was thinking, among other things, of the sixth-century poet and musician Arion.

30. It is interesting and surely significant that the Dorians did not try to exploit the name "tragedy" for their claim. It was too obviously Athenian.

31. These allegations of the "Dorians" are neither true nor to the point. "Comedy" is from *kômos*, 'revel,' an Attic word, not from *kômê*, 'village,' and *drân* is not an exclusively Doric word (it is true that *prattein* is Ionic and Attic).

32. An almost identical statement in the *Parts of Animals* 1, 5, 645a11, suggests that Aristotle may have in mind diagrams or replicas of human and animal bodies for teaching purposes.

33. A squid, an antelope, or whatever. The connecting of the individual with the species is the crux of the matter.

34. Aristotle means simply that a dactylic verse (*metron*) is a segment six "feet" or measures long, cut out of an indefinite continuum of dactylically shaped speech, etc.

35. Here a short section of text (three lines long in the original) has been transposed. It will be found at the beginning of the following paragraph: "Now it happens . . . poems of that sort."

36. Aristotle does not mean that iambic verse was low or comic in itself, but that since the lampooning was give-and-take, the metre that was closest in rhythm to the back-and-forth of speech (see 49a24) was chosen as its medium. (We learn in sec. 21, 59b31-37, that the hexameter verse came similarly to be used for epic because it is weighty and, as it were, stationary, hence best suited to the early hymns and encomia which were devoted in good part to a leisurely *narrative* of heroic deeds.) However, the activity of "flyting" or lampooning, *iambizein*, ended by giving its name to the verse. Cf. the aetiological story of the maid Iambe in the "Homeric" *Hymn to Demeter*, lines 195 ff.

37. Literally, "some of the early people became poets (i.e., makers) of epic. , . . ." *Poets*, actual makers of poems, now appear for the first time, as distinguished from the improvisers who imitated but did not "build."

38. Cf. sec. 24, 60a5-11. To Aristotle, "poet" and "poetic" do not connote sensitive imagery or sensuous language but dramatic strength and directness of presentation.

39. I.e., through the pioneering work of Homer as sketched in the preceding paragraph—not in the improvisations mentioned below, lines 10-13. An important part of Aristotle's theory of the origins of the dramatic genres, tragedy and comedy, is that their "forms" or

essences were grasped and foreshadowed by Homer before they actually came into being as genres.

40. Inserting the relative pronoun *ho* (one letter in Greek) enables us to keep the verb "is (can be) judged."

41. The phrase used here, *allos logos*, is normally, in Aristotle's usage, a signal that the "other story" will be taken up in due time; and indeed this question is taken up at the end of our *Poetics*, in sec. 26; for the question is essentially whether tragedy is *so much better* (at their mutually shared purpose: cf. 62b14) *than the epic.* Usually it is thought that Aristotle is asking here whether tragedy has "by now," i.e., in his time, reached its highest possible development—a question which never appears again in the *Poetics*.

42. The word *phallika*, which is taken for granted in most editions and translations, has no substantial manuscript support. Aristotle may just possibly have written *phaula*, 'low-class'; most of the MSS have *phaulika*, a nonsense word.

43. Thus Aristotle is an evolutionist in the history of human culture, though not in natural history. Cf. *Sophistical Refutations*, 34, 183b22-34.

44. In other words, to the canonical size for the tragic troupe, which remained permanently at one leading actor and two supporting players. Usually Aristotle's remark is taken as referring simply to the "second actor" in a general sense: i.e., the second of the three. See also the following note.

45. Here two—I think it is two rather than one, although they run continuously—short clauses are omit-

ted. So far as they can be interpreted (the text of the second at least appears to have been disturbed), they appear to say: "and three (*sc.* actors) and scene-painting (*sc.* were introduced) by Sophocles. Furthermore, with respect to (?) its grandeur (? size ?), out of petty (short?) plots, and ludicrous diction, thanks to having developed out of a *satyrikon* (satyr-play?) it turned serious late." My chief reason for omitting this farrago, aside from the difficulty of eliciting sense from it (a difficulty which is glossed over by most of the editors and commentators), is that it breaks into and destroys the overall rationale of Aristotle's passage, which has to do with the victory of "speech," i.e., dialogue, *in Aeschylus*, and the consequent victory of iambic verse. If the omitted clauses are genuine, or if either one of them is, they (it) can be tolerated only as a parenthesis.

46. Nothing in this clause (the one in the omitted passage *may* be different) makes it necessary to assume that Aristotle is talking about an actual satyr-drama with a chorus of satyrs.

47. At this point our Greek texts carry the names of two comic poets, Epicharmus and Phormis (elsewhere spelled Phormos), but not in construction with the rest of the sentence. The Arabic version offers instead an enigmatic phrase, with no trace of the two names. They are fairly clearly an intrusive note; which is not to say that Aristotle was not thinking of these poets.—In line a34 above ("the ugly, of which . . .") I read *toû aischroû, hoû* (this word not in Kassel's text).

48. Not "agrees with," but in the full temporal sense of the aorist indicative. The language implies a

figure: epic poetry is an attendant or satellite who "stayed with" his lord, Tragedy, for a certain distance on his journey but did not go the whole way.—The following two lines in the translation are based on a text which differs from Kassel's: namely *mechri men toû metrôi megalê mimêsis eînai.* . . .

49. Not "to represent the events of" a single day. Traditionally applied to the "dramatic day," the time assumed to elapse during the play; I take it of the actual length of the respective poems, and therefore of the respective performances.—This passage is of course the root of the Renaissance "Unity of Time."

50. I have chosen this relatively colorless term for what are literally the "six parts of tragedy." The important thing to remember is that they are elements or stages in the art and process (see note 1) of making tragedies rather than parts of *a* tragedy.

51. So far as comedy is concerned this is a reference to the lost second book. See Introduction, p. 10.

52. After considerable hesitation I have left the last clause ("through a course . . . characteristics") in the text, although it was bracketed in my previous book. Every other clause in the definition is "recovered," as Aristotle says, from what has been said previously; only this one is, so far as we can see, entirely new. The crucial novelty in my interpretation is that the word *pathêmatôn,* usually translated "feelings" or the like, is taken as the plural form of the technical term *pathos* (as it is in sec. 23, 59b11; for *pathos* itself see sec. 12, 52b10) and therefore means "tragic acts." In what

sense and what way these are purified can be formulated better when we come to secs. 13 and 14.

53. I follow Bywater in referring this term (*opsis*, 'vision, sight, appearance') to the appearance of the *persons*, i.e., their masks and costumes, rather than to the stage setting in general.

54. Not the versification as such, but the composition of the verses as a whole, i.e., the clothing of them in suitable language.

55. Unfortunately it is not entirely clear to us, who lack the music of the plays and know desperately little about Greek music anyway. The crucial point I would argue for is that under "song-composition" Aristotle includes both the music and the words of the songs.

56. The awkwardness of the terminology is regrettable but cannot be helped. "Actors" means, for better or worse, the living individuals who are hired to play the parts, whereas Aristotle means the *persons of the play* as such, as they are projected in the poet's text before casting begins.

57. Tragedy as a whole genre or species, not any particular play as a whole.

58. I omit an interpolated (as I consider it) subject of the verb: "not a few of them, more or less" (the expression is crude, perhaps corrupted), and, following "use," another list of the six "parts." Its purpose, even its connection with the preceding passage, is unclear, and the order appears to be even more random than before: "for in fact the whole (?) contains visual appear-

ance(s?) and character and plot and verbal expression and song and thought in the same way (?!)."

59. At this point I follow Kassel in omitting a sentence which most editors try to integrate with the text (usually by inserting "and of happiness" before it): "Both happiness and unhappiness are in action, and the goal is a certain action, not a quality." Kassel also omits the following clause ("and they have . . . with their actions"), which I think is essential to Aristotle's argument.—I take Aristotle's *biou* and *praxeôs* here to refer not to Life and Action in the large, but to the life and action of a particular individual. The word *praxis* has this focus in it by implication from the beginning (i.e., not merely in Aristotle): a single *course* of action laid on by a particular will to achieve a particular goal (cf. sec. 11, 51a18). The reversal of a focused, unitary intention, in which the whole life of a man may be concentrated, is at the very heart of tragedy as Aristotle conceives it.

60. I follow Castelvetro in transposing this sentence from a short distance below, just after ". . . the characters come second."

61. Aristotle appears to be guilty of some wavering in his view of "thought." Previously (sec. 9, 50a6) and just below (50b11) it is defined "topologically," as a certain kind of passage in a play; here it is a certain faculty or ability (*to . . . dynasthai*). A similar wobbling between inner and outer criteria appears in the definitions of "character(s)." One cardinal point seems clear, however: "thought" does not exist in a play unless the characters express it in speech.

62. Three words are omitted here which say "in the

case of (i.e., this pertains to?) the speeches." They seem to be, in origin, a marginal note or tag.

63. One might paraphrase the two adverbs by "like men and citizens" and "like conscious speech-makers."

64. A clause is omitted here which appears to be a doublet or variant of part of what stands in the parenthesis. The clause reads: "in which (or, in things in which) it is not clear whether (?) one is choosing or rejecting."

65. I.e., in scientific or mathematical discussions.

66. The speeches are contrasted (*men . . . de*) with the choral songs ("the remaining parts," 50b15).

67. See sec. 9, 49b28.

68. These two phrases seem to designate animate creatures and inanimate (created) structures respectively.

69. Omitting a short phrase: "(is) not of (does not belong to) the art."

70. The text is uncertain and there is no other record of such a period.

71. This "norm" should be compared with the formulation of the so-called "unity of time," sec. 8, 49b12-14.

72. This statement poses a problem, because the incident of the wounding on Parnassus *is* told in our *Odyssey*, and at some length, 19, 392-466. The answer presumably is that it is not told for its own sake or in its own order (i.e., as part of the main story) but as an "episode" in quite another context, to account for the

scar which Eurycleia recognizes in the foot-washing scene.

73. It is surely significant that what happens to a man is mentioned only under the heading of particulars, while the "universals" include only what he himself says or does. There is a certain brutal arbitrariness and finality about a tragic *happening*, very different from the representative quality of what the hero says or does in response to it.

74. Aristotle, as a classical Greek, takes it for granted that Greek mythology reflects history, i.e., that its heroes actually existed. He was probably right in many, perhaps a great many, cases.

75. This whole piece of reasoning is a "paralogism" which Aristotle is anxious to expose.

76. Observe that the poet is a poet, i.e., a *maker*, through his *imitations*. The paradox appears to be intentional.

77. Simple plots and actions are not defined until the third paragraph below (old chap. 10). Aristotle not infrequently operates in this backward fashion (cf. peripety and recognition just below); nothing is out of order here.

78. It is not entirely clear whether Aristotle means excessive lengthening (padding) of a short plot, or excessive straining of the sequence of events, or both.

79. The Greek word (*peplegmenos*) means literally something like "inwoven, intricate"; such a plot is woven into and upon itself.

80. Aristotle is referring to sec. 11, and especially to the sentence on the "norm of length," 51a12-15.—Just below in line 17 ("the reversal is continuous"), I read *hês hexês* instead of *ex hês*.

81. Again a reference to 51a12-15. But "what is being undertaken" implies that the events do not just "happen," as was intimated there, but are initiated by the hero with a certain purpose in mind—a purpose which is then frustrated by the outcome.

82. All that we know about this play by Aristotle's friend Theodectes is what we learn in this passage and in sec. 18, 55b29-32.

83. Sec. 9, 49b27 and sec. 12, 52a2-3.

84. The *pathos* is the foundation stone of the tragic structure. Its emotional potentialities will be explored in sec. 14. Peripety and recognition are limited to complex plots, indeed they constitute the definition of a complex plot. The *pathos*, on the other hand, can equally well be embodied in a simple plot (e.g., the *Medea*; see below, sec. 14, 53b27-29). In fact it appears that the happening *or threatened happening* (see n. 101 below) of a *pathos* is the *sine qua non* of all tragedy.

85. All of chapter 12 (according to the conventional numbering) except this first clause is excluded from the translation as spurious. Its feeble and repetitive definitions reek of some late *grammatikos*. A translation will be found in the Appendix, A, p. 76.

86. This has been implied rather than said in the foregoing. If the particular work or "job" of tragedy is to arouse pity and fear, and if peripety and recognition

are as effective in arousing them as has just been claimed (sec. 12, 52a38ff.), then the complex plot is the kind one wants.

87. In what follows only three, not four, patterns are mentioned. Aristotle presumably thought that the fourth possible pattern, a shift of the good man from bad to good fortune, was too obviously untragic to need mentioning.

88. *To philanthrôpon*. The most natural, i.e., the least forced interpretation of this much discussed term is that it denotes a rudimentary grade of pity which is accorded to all human beings (*anthrôpoi*) regardless of their deserts, whereas pity (*eleos*) depends on a judgment that the sufferer does not deserve his misfortune.

89. These two men may be the same man: i.e., pity and fear *can* be excited by (or for) the same individual.

90. Here a sentence is omitted: "Most (or, And most) of his (*sc.* plays) end unhappily."

91. I.e., as those who favored a "double" structure, with good fortune for the good and bad for the bad; see just above, 53a13, and below, a31-33.

92. Lit. "appear": i.e., to audiences. Cf. below, 53a30; sec. 14, 53b14; sec. 19, 56b5.

93. A sentence is omitted here as an interpolation: "For there (*sc.* in comedy), even if they are (omitting the article *hoi*) implacable enemies in the story, like Orestes and Aegisthus, they end by walking off as friends, and nobody gets killed by anybody."

94. Sec. 13 dealt with overall plot patterns, centering in the "shift" or change of fortune and considered

in conjunction with the moral quality of the hero(es). Sec. 14 takes up the possible varieties of *tragic act* (*pathos*) and their relative potentialities for tragic feeling, considered in conjunction with the *blood relationship* or lack of it between the doer and the sufferer of the tragic deed (the *pathos*).

95. Aristophanes jeers repeatedly at Euripides' beggar-king Telephus, who aroused the commiseration of the heroes—and the audience—by appearing in rags. See esp. *Acharnians* 428-446. There is a tradition (*Life of Aeschylus*) that some spectators fainted with fear at the dreadful appearance of the Furies in the *Eumenides*.

96. Aristotle seems to mean the *bare* plot, not yet clothed in speeches, verses, images, etc. But I take it that he has in mind the plot structure *as shaped by the poet*: in other words, that he does indeed mean "the plot of the *Oedipus*," not simply "the story of Oedipus."—The mention of *shuddering* with fear suggests that the fear Aristotle has in mind is a species of horror, or is closely related to horror. See note 101.

97. Murders or intended murders involving close blood kin evoke the tragic emotions most powerfully. There is something faintly ghoulish about the calm with which Aristotle identifies these situations as the ones "one should look for," but the remark is consistent with his theory. What he is talking about is in fact—whether he himself is aware of this is not clear—one of the most primitive and potent taboos in all human cultures, that against the shedding of kindred blood. Such a killing brings on the doer a "pollution" almost too fearsome to bear. Archaic Greece worked hard to exorcise these

ghosts, with Apollo of Delphi and his prescribed round of ritual purifications as its chief agent. But documents like the *Oresteia* and the *Oedipus King* for the fifth century, and the so-called *Tetralogies* of the orator Antiphon or the ninth book of Plato's *Laws* for the fourth, show how powerful and deep-seated the old horror of blood pollution still was, even in the minds of highly educated men. The tragic *pathos* is by preference to be charged with this kind of explosive emotional force.

98. The word translated here "artistic" is the adverb *kalôs*, lit. "beautifully." Cf. sec. 13, 52b31, "the finest tragedy," lit. "the most beautiful"; 53a22, "the technically finest tragedy," lit. "the according-to-the-art most beautiful." But the artistic "beauty" of a tragedy consists not in some prettiness or decoration applied to it from outside, but in the cogency and elegance (in the sense in which mathematicians use the term) with which the plot structure is shaped to combine *logical sequence* with *shattering emotional impact*. Cf. sec. 12, 52a4; sec. 14, 54a4. It is, in a real sense, a functional beauty.

99. This sentence has been inserted here, following Gudeman and others, because it is required by the scheme, is referred to below (53b37-38), and seems to be implied by the Arabic version.

100. Suppressing the word "third," which appears in the manuscripts at this point.

101. In *Aristotle's Poetics: The Argument*, pp. 423-47, I have argued that the word *miaron*, here translated "morally repulsive character" (lit. "the filthy" or "polluted"; cf. sec. 13, 52b36), is a clue—an unobtrusive

one, it must be admitted—to Aristotle's theory of the tragic catharsis. According to that argument, the "catharsis" is a purification of whatever is "filthy" or "polluted" in the *pathos*, the tragic act. If we may judge by the present passage, the "filthiness" inheres in a conscious intention to kill a person who is close kin (father, brother, etc.). An *unconscious* intention to do so, i.e., an intention to do so without being aware of the kinship—as Oedipus did not know that the old man he killed at the crossroads was his father—would therefore be "pure," *katharos*. But the purity must be established to our satisfaction. *Catharsis* would then be the process of proving that the act was pure in that sense. How is such a thing proved? According to the *Nicomachean Ethics* 3, 2, 1110b19 and 1111a20, by the remorse of the doer, which shows that if he had known the facts he would not have done the deed. In the *Oedipus*, the thing which establishes this to our satisfaction is Oedipus' self-blinding. It, then, effects a "purification" of the tragic deed and so makes Oedipus eligible for our pity (as well as our "fear"; i.e., our horror: see note 97).—The usual interpretations of "catharsis" are far too numerous to list here, but they all, or almost all, have in common a focus on the pity and fear which are aroused *in the spectator*. These are to be somehow either "purified" (reduced to beneficent order and proportion) or "purged" (expelled from his emotional system) by the play. Such interpretations are not sustained so much by anything in the *Poetics* itself as by a passage in the *Politics*, 8, 7, 1341b38, which speaks of a musical "catharsis" in comparable terms and refers to "the *Poetics*" (not the extant portion, obviously) for the definitive discussion. The basic question is whether we are to think of literature as a therapeutic device, and the spectator—or reader—as a patient to be treated.

102. Aristotle mentions this case in the *Nicomachean Ethics* 3, 1, 1111a11, as an example of an error of fact: Merope thinks her son is an enemy.

103. Omitting a conjunction (*gar*) which cannot be translated.

104. Sec. 10, 50b9.

105. The text is very uncertain here. Kassel's full text would be translated "but it is not appropriate to a woman to be brave or clever in that way"; but there is no clue to help us interpret the reference "in that way."

106. Melanippe, in one of Euripides' two plays by that name, showed great cleverness in a set speech; but a woman has no business being clever.

107. Aristotle is referring to Iphigenia's two "big" speeches, *Iphigenia at Aulis* 1211-1252 and 1368-1401.

108. I read *êthous* rather than *mythou*, which Kassel prints.

109. The "machine" (*mêchanê*) was of course simply a hand-operated crane which could hoist a god, or occasionally another key person, onto the roof of the stage building for a more-than-mortal appearance. The use of a *deus ex machina* to unravel a tangled plot was particularly characteristic of Euripides. Medea plays a variation on the role at the end of her tragedy.

110. The manuscripts give "*Iliad*," but there is no actual sailing of the fleet in the *Iliad* (including Book 2), and no *deus ex machina*. Neither is there one of the

latter in the *Iphigenia at Aulis* as we have it, but in another version known to us, and the one with which Aristotle probably was acquainted, Artemis did play that role.

111. Two brief phrases are omitted here: (1) "in the case of the characters" or "applying to their characters" (just after "traits of that kind"), and (2) "example of hardness" (just before the name "Achilles," and supposedly referring to him). Just before "Homer" I have inserted the word *homoion*, "like" (*sc.* other men). —The last three lines of old chap. 15 are here attached to the beginning of sec. 17; see below.

112. Although there is no reason to suspect the genuineness of this section, it is a later addition to the text of the *Poetics* which has been arbitrarily stuck in just here (landing in the process between two parts of the same sentence; see note 120). But it will not fit any better elsewhere.

113. Sec. 12, 52a29-32.

114. A birthmark which according to tradition was found on all the *Spartoi* or "Sown Men," a group of Theban aristocrats descended from those who sprang from the dragon's teeth sown by Cadmus.—I have not attempted to document all the following allusions. In the case of those to lost plays, we often know little or nothing more than what is said here.

115. *Odyssey* 19. 386-475 and 21. 205-225. In the first case the scar is seen by Eurycleia through a kind of peripety, i.e., an accident but a natural one; in the other, Odysseus deliberately points to it to prove his identity.

116. At the end of the preceding paragraph.

117. I.e., the web through which Philomela revealed to her sister what had happened.

118. My translation sticks as close as possible to Aristotle's words, but unfortunately the clue to his allusions is lost.

119. This section deals with three main problems that face the poet in the process of "writing out" his play: (1) certain basic perceptions of the characters: i.e., of their location, what they are doing, and the like; (2) the rendering of the characters' feelings into the right kinds ("forms") of language; and (3) the right proportion of length as between basic text and episodes. For this latter purpose the poet should draw up an outline of the plot in general terms.

120. This phrase (from the end of old chap. 15) must refer to perceptions of a different order from the visual quality of a mask or a costume: some kind of visual effect *inherent* in the nature of poetry, i.e., of drama, since the drama is the natural and final condition of poetry. The discussion of such perceptions begins in the sentence that immediately follows (formerly cut in two by sec. 16). It seems, then, that the *Poetics* offers a skeleton treatment of the question, but for more detail the reader is to consult the dialogue *On Poets* (which is almost certainly the "published discourses"; see Introduction, p. 9).

121. Not "figures of speech" solely or exclusively, in the usual sense of the phrase, although such figures are included. It is more generally a question of the modes

or shapes, as it were, which language naturally takes on under the stress of strong emotion. For a clue to what Aristotle means see *Rhetoric* 3, 7, 1408a10 ff.

122. I now prefer this reading to *mâllon ê*, "more than, rather than," but either could be defended. Perhaps the most significant thing is that the question of poetic inspiration, which is so important in Plato (see Introduction, p. 5), receives only this oblique and fleeting mention in the *Poetics*.

123. *Epeisodioûn*, 'episodize.' There is a possible ambiguity here. *Epeisodion* (from *epeisodos*) was originally a term that belonged specifically to the drama, designating a new scene as marked by the entrance of a new character ("Enter to them So-and-so"). In that sense every scene in a drama is an "episode," and one might expect that simple meaning here. But the "episodes" of the *Iphigenia*, 55b14-15, and even more clearly those of the *Odyssey*, 55b23, are *extra* scenes added on to the central story (the "general"), and so that sense must be intended here also. Cf. the "episodic" plot, sec. 12, 51b33; sec. 18, 56a2.

124. A phrase—actually a pair of phrases—is omitted here: "For what cause—outside of the abstract."

125. The words "his sister" have survived in the Arabic version. On the other hand I omit here a compound clause which in my opinion has intruded into the text (see *Aristotle's Poetics: The Argument*, pp. 508-10): "whether the way Euripides or the way Polyidus composed it, namely as a result of his saying naturally enough: 'So then, not only my sister but I was destined to be sacrificed.'" The clause is based on the words in sec.

16, 55a5-8, above: "And the one suggested . . . it is my turn," but with the mistaken idea that Polyidus was a dramatist (he was actually a sophist, i.e., a critic) who composed (*epoiêsen*) a different recognition from Euripides'. Anyhow the manner of the recognition is no part of the "abstract."

126. Omitting the preposition *en*, 'in,' which would make Aristotle refer to the play *Orestes*.

127. I believe that the name "Poseidon" is a gloss which has replaced "a god." Proper names, of gods or men, do not belong in an outline like this. Odysseus is merely "a certain man" at this stage.

128. It must be admitted that "tying" and "untying" are not very elegant words, but they are more exact than any others I can think of. "Dénouement" has been borrowed into English without a partner, whereas the correlation is Aristotle's most important point; and anyhow its scope is too restricted: it is normally used only of the very end of a play ("end of the last act"), whereas Aristotle's *lysis* starts much farther back.—There are indications that the first two paragraphs of this section are a later addition by Aristotle, and "tying" and "untying" represent a new element in his theory. It is very likely, however, that they were technical terms of the theatre which Aristotle adopted.

129. I now follow Bywater in thinking that the sentence is probably complete. The Greek says simply "of them," but it is hardly possible that anyone else is meant than Lynceus and Hypermestra. The child would be their son Abas. For a free-wheeling conjecture as to the course of the plot see my *Aristotle's Poetics: The Argu-*

ment, pp. 521-22. The only thing certain is that it was complex and Danaus was somehow hoist by his own petard (see sec. 12, 52a27-29).

130. This statement is a well-known *crux*, since there is no previous list of just four "parts" (tragedy had six, sec. 9, 50a8, and the tragic plot had three, sec. 12, 52b9-10). Character (the "moral" kind) is one of the six "parts," the *pathos* ("fatal") is one of the three, and the complex kind, being "all peripety and recognition," accounts for the other two "parts of the plot." More significant is the fact that the four key concepts have been discussed, *in the order used here*, in the four preceding sections (sec. 16 being a later addition): complex plot, sec. 13; *pathos*, sec. 14; characters, sec. 15; episodes, sec. 17.—The inexactness of the reference is perhaps mitigated if this paragraph also is a later addition by Aristotle (see note 128).

131. Substituting "and the episodic" for "and the fourth kind *oes*." In place of these three meaningless letters, many editors and translators have accepted Bywater's conjecture *opsis* and made the fourth kind of tragedy the "spectacular."

132. "Hades" might suggest to us a high tragic theme, but that does not seem to have been its connotation in the later fifth and the fourth century. We know of a number of Hades plays from that period, and they were all comedies or satyr-dramas. The common trait of all such plays (derived, presumably, from Book 11 of the *Odyssey*) is their "episodic" character: they consist of a series of interviews with the great dead.

133. Aristotle has not previously enunciated the warning that follows ("not to make an epic mass into a

tragedy"), but he *has* repeatedly pointed to the thing which is the basis for that warning, namely the special character of tragedy with respect to length: sec. 8, 49b12-14; sec. 11, 51a12-15; sec. 17, 55b15-16; cf. further sec. 24, 59b17-28.

134. The notion of dramatizing or "composing" a story "whole" seems to be related to the concept of plot or story which appears earlier in this section, namely that some of it (part of the "tying") may be outside the poem. The "story of the *Iliad*," incorporated into a poem in anything like its full scope, might indeed be very long. See sec. 23, 59a32.

135. Reading *Hekabên* with Giorgio Valla instead of *Niobên* with the manuscripts, and putting no *ê* before the name. Most versions of the text make Aristotle commend Euripides and Aeschylus in parallel with each other for having handled the problem correctly.

136. Here a short sentence is omitted: "For this is tragic and 'philanthropic.' " In his previous mention of the "philanthropic," Aristotle distinguished it sharply from the tragic: sec. 13, 53a1-4.—The "marvelous effects" which the dramatic poets (i.e., those of Aristotle's day) were aiming at may have included some of the irrational happenings which come off better in the epic, not only because of its length but because of its narrative character: sec. 24, 60a12-17. Aristotle seems to be suggesting to these poets that there are varieties of the marvelous which are more consonant with the nature of tragedy: e.g., a peripety like the "fooling" of Sisyphus.

137. It should be noted that Aristotle says nothing about the "thought" of the choral odes, which is so

important to us (e.g., the "Through suffering, learning" of the *Agamemnon* or the "Many are the wonders" ode of the *Antigone*). He considers the choral parts solely under the heading of "musical composition," which he said, sec. 10, 50b16, is "the greatest of the sensuous attractions." His purpose here seems to be to remind the dramatists of his own day of its importance *with the public*, as a contributory factor to success in the competitions.

138. To be distinguished, of course, from the pity and fear which it is the business of the tragic *pathos* (sec. 14), or of the play as a whole, to arouse *in the spectator* (or reader). Pity and fear here are emotions which one dramatic character sets out to arouse in another through the artful use of speech.

139. Here a phrase is omitted, saying literally "and also bigness and smallnesses." What it means is the general *topos* or topic which consists in trying to persuade the listener of the importance or unimportance of a given thing. But this is already included in the general heading "proof and refutation."

140. The analysis of language which follows is of interest chiefly for what it reveals about the state of linguistic theory in Aristotle's day—though it is possible that it, or parts of it, represent a later enlargement of Aristotle's text by someone else in the school who had taken over the "poetics course": see Introduction, p. 9.

141. The author makes the mistake that comes so naturally to literate people who are just beginning to reflect on language: that of partially confusing the writing system with the speech system which it represents.

On the whole, however, considering that the formal analysis of language had only begun in the fifth century, with sophists like Protagoras (whose efforts were mentioned so slightingly just above), what is offered here already shows a respectable degree of sophistication.

142. All these matters are important for the preservation and interpretation of *poetic texts*, especially the great national texts like *Iliad* and *Odyssey*; and it was out of that concern that formal grammar came in Greece, as it did in India and elsewhere. Hence the "metrician's" task is more comprehensive and more important than merely to analyze the "metres" of poetry; he is the counterpart, in Aristotle's language, of what is later called simply the *grammatikos*.

143. Here I follow Bywater's revision of the text, which stretches as far as "or in the middle" (under the "article"); but everything is very uncertain. In any case the category translated "conjunction" (*syndesmos*, a ligament, or 'that which binds together') does not exactly coincide with what we call by that name.

144. "Noun" includes the adjective (first distinguished from the noun by the Stoic grammarians of the second century B.C.), some pronouns, and even the definite article.

145. A very broad concept, covering any modification undergone by any word capable of inflection, and including the modern categories of case, number, tense, etc.,: e.g., *anthrôpos*, *anthrôpeios*, *anthrôpeiôs*, "man (human being), human, humanly"; *badizei*, *ebadize*, *ebadise*, "he is walking, he was walking, he walked (once)."

146. As in the following section (22) on poetic style, Aristotle's theory is based on the notion of the *regular or standard word* (the *kyrion*), which can then be replaced, transferred (metaphor), or modified. In other words poetic language is not a special kind of language directly attuned to its subject, but ordinary language heightened, altered, or decorated in order to raise it above the ordinary and make a "poetic" impression on the hearer.

147. At this point a lacuna in the manuscripts has swallowed up the discussion of *kosmos*, the ornamental word.

148. The following eight or nine lines, on certain features of gender in nouns, have nothing to do with the subject of poetic language and are most probably an interpolation by some late person of "grammatical" character (cf. old chap. 12). A translation is given in the Appendix, B, p. 77. (Lines 58b8-10, shortly below, appear in the Appendix, C.)

149. The reference, for which cf. Aristotle *Rhetoric* 3, 2, 1405a35, is to what in more modern times was called a "cupping-glass," an instrument for bleeding patients. In antiquity it was often made of bronze, and was heated to improve its "set."

150. The alliteration in the English version ("feasts on the flesh of my foot") is fortuitous and has no connection with Aristotle's point. What follows is relegated to the Appendix, D, p. 78.

151. In view of what follows, the poetry "which is narrative and works in verse" is perhaps meant to be

contrasted with history, which is narrative but works in prose.

152. See sec. 11. Aristotle seems to have in mind here both the unified living creature (*zôion*) and the entity composed of parts (inorganic structure), which were distinguished from one another there. Either can be well put together and thus produce the aesthetic pleasure special to poetry. Whether the specific pleasure appropriate to *tragedy*, i.e., based on pity and fear (sec. 14, 53b11), is also appropriate to the epic, and to all epics, is not quite clear, though from the remark at the end of the *Poetics*, sec. 26, 62b13-14, it would seem that it is.

153. Sec. 11, 51a23ff.

154. Cf. sec. 18, 56a10-15.

155. I.e., any more than he put everything that happened to Odysseus during his life into the *Odyssey*: sec. 11, 51a23-25.

156. *Dialambanei* is usually translated by "diversifies" or some such word. But Aristotle's point here is not, as it is below (sec. 24, 59b30), the relief of monotony, but the lengthening effect of the episodes, which are inserted as it were between the joints or limbs of the central plot and "hold them apart." This is in fact very much the way the *Iliad* is constructed: central action, Books 1 (Quarrel), 9 (Embassy), 16-17 (Patrocleia), etc., with "episodes" filling the interstices.

157. Here an interpolated note is omitted, listing the plays that have been—or could be?—drawn from the *Little Iliad*. The note has suffered interpolation in turn:

"Eight [more], such as *Award of the Arms, Philoctetes, Neoptolemus, Eurypylus, Begging Expedition, Laconian Women, Sack of Troy,* and *Departure of the Fleet* [also *Sinon* and *Trojan Women*]."

158. Usually translated "must have," "necessarily has," or the like. But Aristotle's point is precisely that most epics do *not* follow his prescription. Homer is the only epic poet who knows his business: sec. 24, 60a5.

159. A phrase is omitted, saying "outside of song-composition and visual adornment." Whoever wrote these words thought that the "parts" referred to here were the six constituent elements of sec. 9.

160. The word translated "tragic acts" is *pathê-matôn*, used as genitive plural of the word *pathos* that appeared in sec. 12, 52b10.

161. Sec. 11, 51a11-15.

162. Whether or not Aristotle has in mind connected trilogies like the *Oresteia*, the bulk he suggests would come to 4500 lines, or less than a third the length of the *Iliad* (conventionally reckoned as 15,693 lines, the *Odyssey* as 12,105). But most early epics were actually much shorter than that; few exceeded 5000 lines. —There is an obvious discrepancy between the statements in the text. Aristotle seems to mean that it would be desirable to have epics approximate the length of tragedy—or of the tragic trilogy—but that that is not possible because they have a special license to exceed the limit by adding "episodes" of indefinite number and bulk. If an epic did follow Aristotle's recommendation, then, would it cease to be an epic? (It is thought that

the Hellenistic poet Apollonius Rhodius followed the recommendation in limiting his epic *Argonautica* to four books.)

163. The crucial feature of this translation is the phrase "as of the time they are enacted." Dramatic presentation establishes the here-and-now of whatever is being currently played on the stage as the master time-focus, whereas to the narrative poet all times are equally close and available. Traditionally, the passage has been read as speaking of the "unity of place," though not necessarily in the sense of a mandatory rule.

164. Here two short phrases are omitted, the first immediately following "this virtue" and the second immediately following "diversifying": "for (purposes of) magnificence," and "(for) | diverting [here the basic meaning of the verb has to be stretched] the spectator."

165. "Them" must mean no more, but also no less, than the three chief stichic or spoken verses: dactylic hexameter, iambic trimeter, trochaic tetrameter. Chaeremon's *Centaur* was mentioned in sec. 2, 47b21-22.

166. Cf. sec. 11, 51b27-32.

167. *Odyssey* 21. From the "stranger's" correct description of Odysseus' dress on the way to Troy, 221ff., Penelope draws the false conclusion that this man once entertained her husband (rather than that he *is* her husband). A man who had entertained Odysseus would be able to describe him; this man is able to describe him; *ergo*, ...

168. This section is not really a part of the fabric of the *Poetics*. It appears to be a compendium of material

collected and published elsewhere and simply tacked on here, possibly by a later redactor, as an appendix to Aristotle's discussion of the epic. Homeric (or epic; but they were in fact mostly Homeric) "problems" were a popular parlor game and literary genre as early as the fifth century, consisting of various charges or allegations against the poet, often of the most nitpicking variety, and suggested lines of defense. The point of view in sec. 25 is that of an attorney working up a brief. It is noteworthy that very little of what is said in it has anything in common with Aristotle's main theory of poetry. There are some signs that it may originally have antedated the *Poetics.*

169. The argument is essentially against Plato, who made a great point of the "correctness" (*orthotês*) and "incorrectness" of poetry (see, e.g., *Republic* 10, 601d-e; *Laws* 2, 653b-6602), and always on the assumption that it must be judged by the same criteria as political or moral questions.

170. Of course the "pacing" horse does precisely this. In this case, if nature has not imitated art, at least art anticipated second nature. We do not know whether Aristotle was uninformed or the invention had not yet been made in Greece.

171. It is perhaps of interest that our texts of Homer do not show the word "all" before "gods." Aristotle, like most Greeks, usually quotes his Homer from memory, and sometimes gets it wrong. It is of course possible that he knew a text which did have "all."

172. I.e., an irrational assumption as to what the text under consideration means.

173. This much of the sentence is missing in the Greek text.

174. Reading *enantion*, as tentatively suggested by Kassel.

175. The notion of a *synkrisis*, a comparative rating of epic and tragedy, was perhaps suggested to Aristotle by a passage in Plato's *Laws*, 2.658d-e (or by oral discussions in the Academy of which that passage is the precipitate), where tragedy is rated below the epic. The judgment makes sense for Plato: the two genres are equally far removed from the truth about human life, but tragedy, being the more direct and immediate in its method, is the more harmful. Aristotle emphasizes the directness and immediacy even more than Plato does (cf. sec. 4, 48a21-22; sec. 9, 49b26-27; here, 62a17-18), but since there is no question of poetry presenting a metaphysical view of human life in competition with some other more "correct" one, its greater vividness can be reckoned as a merit rather than a defect.

176. I read *dêlon an eiê* instead of the *aei, lian dêlon* which Kassel prints.

177. It is especially evident here that we have a series of jottings, some of which hardly make full sentences.

178. It is not clear how this item differs from no. 3.

179. I omit the phrases "and the *Odyssey*" and, a line or so below, "and some (other) poems of that kind" (or, with a slight change of text, "and yet these poems").

180. See sec. 14, 53b11-13; sec. 23, 59a21.

181. On the last page of manuscript B these words are followed by some traces which may be remnants of "but concerning iambics and comedy . . . ." The reading is not certain, but in any case, as was said in the Introduction (p. 10), there is little doubt that the *Poetics* originally had a second book. Furthermore the sentence translated here "Well then, . . ." begins with a pair of particles, *men oun*, which is Aristotle's normal way of signifying that he is finishing one topic and proceeding to the next.

SELECT BIBLIOGRAPHY

NOTE: The following list gives a rigidly limited selection out of the enormous literature on the *Poetics*. It tries to do no more than suggest to the inquiring student a few places where he may begin some further reading.

I. GREEK TEXT

Aristotelis De Arte Poetica Liber, (ed.) Rudolf(us) Kassel. Oxford 1965 (Oxford Classical Texts).

II. GREEK TEXT WITH TRANSLATION AND NOTES

Ingram Bywater, *Aristotle on the Art of Poetry*. Oxford 1909.

Samuel H. Butcher, *Aristotle's Theory of Poetry and Fine Art*. 4th ed., London 1932 (essays take the place of a commentary). Greek text and translation published separately as *The Poetics of Aristotle*. 4th ed., London 1922. The translation also republished by Hill and Wang, with introduction by Francis Fergusson, New York 1961.

J. Hardy, *Aristote Poétique* (in the "Budé" series). Paris 1932 (French transl. and notes).

A. Rostagni, *Aristotele Poetica*. 2d ed., Torino 1945 (no transl., Italian notes).

III. TRANSLATIONS WITH NOTES
(in addition to those mentioned under II)

W. Hamilton Fyfe, *Aristotle, The Poetics* (Loeb Classical Library; with "Longinus" and "Demetrius"). London and New York 1927.

L. J. Potts, *Aristotle on the Art of Fiction*. Cambridge: Cambridge University Press, 1953.

G. M. A. Grube, *Aristotle on Poetry and Style*. New York: The Liberal Arts Press, 1958.

IV. ESSAYS AND INTERPRETATIONS

J. Vahlen, *Beiträge zu Aristoteles Poetik*, 2d printing superv. by H. Schöne, Leipzig 1914 (fundamental work).

Daniel de Montmollin, *La Poétique d'Aristote: texte primitif et additions ultérieures*. Neuchatel 1951.

Humphrey House, *Aristotle's Poetics: A Course of Eight Lectures*. London: Rupert Hart-Davis, 1956.

G. F. Else, *Aristotle's Poetics: The Argument*. Cambridge (Mass.): Harvard U. Press, 1957.

John Jones, *On Aristotle and Greek Tragedy*. Oxford 1962.

Elder Olson, *Aristotle's "Poetics" and English Literature*. Chicago 1965 (essays by various hands).

V. GENERAL WORKS ON ARISTOTLE

W. D. (Sir David) Ross, *Aristotle*. London 1923 (5th ed. repr. 1960; New York: Meridian Books, 1960).

Werner Jaeger, *Aristotle: Fundamentals of the History of His Development*, tr. R. Robinson, Oxford 1934.

VI. FURTHER BIBLIOGRAPHY ON THE *Poetics*

Lane Cooper—Alfred Gudeman, *A Bibliography of the Poetics of Aristotle*. New Haven 1928.

Supplement to the above by Marvin T. Herrick in *American Journal of Philology*, 52 (1931) 168-74.

G. F. Else, "A Survey of Work on Aristotle's Poetics, 1940-1954," *Classical Weekly* (now *Classical World*), 48 (1954-55) 73-82.

INDEX

Abas, 103

Academy, of Plato, 1, 4, 8, 113

Achilles, of Homer, 44, 65

acroamatic works of Aristotle, 8, 10

action(s) (*praxis, eis*), 17, 19, 25–27, 32, 34, 43, 51–52, 61, 64

actors, 29, 34, 40, 51, 64, 73, 87–88, 90–91

adornment, visual, of the characters (*opsis*) (=masks and costumes), 26, 29, 40, 90, 100

Aegeus, in the *Medea*, 72

Aegisthus, in an unknown comedy, 95

Aeschylus, 22, 51, 60, 66, 88

Agathon, 51

Agathon, *Antheus*, 33

Ajax tragedies, 50

Alcmeon, 39, 41

Alexander (the Great), 8

amulets, *see* tokens

Antiphon (the orator), *Tetralogies*, 97

Apollonius Rhodius, *Argonautica*, 110

appropriateness (*to harmotton*), of character, 43

of episodes, 49, 64

Arion, 85

Ariphrades, 78

Aristophanes, 1, 19, 96

Aristotle, see also *Poetics*
acroamatic ("esoteric") works, 8, 10
dialogues (published works), 8, 10
literary interests, 1–2, 112
literary theory, 5–7
On Poets, 9, 85, 101
Rhetoric, 9, 52, 102

Aristoxenus, 9

Artemis, 100

article (*arthron*), 54–55

"artistic(ally)" (*kalos, -ôs*), 15, 29, 38, 41, 45, 63, 69, 97

Assos, in the Troad, 8

astonishing, the; *see* marvelous, the

Astydamas, tragic poet, 41

Athens, Athenian(s), 19, 24

audience, theater, 22, 39, 73

beautiful, the (*to kalon*), 30

beauty of tragedy, 97

beginning, middle(s), and end (*archê, meson(-a), telos*), 30, 61–63

Bekker, I., 14

Ann Arbor Paperbacks

Waddell, *The Desert Fathers*
Erasmus, *The Praise of Folly*
Donne, *Devotions*
Malthus, *Population: The First Essay*
Berdyaev, *The Origin of Russian Communism*
Einhard, *The Life of Charlemagne*
Edwards, *The Nature of True Virtue*
Gilson, *Héloïse and Abélard*
Aristotle, *Metaphysics*
Kant, *Education*
Boulding, *The Image*
Duckett, *The Gateway to the Middle Ages* (3 vols.): *Italy; France and Britain; Monasticism*
Bowditch and Ramsland, *Voices of the Industrial Revolution*
Luxemburg, *The Russian Revolution and Leninism or Marxism?*
Rexroth, *Poems from the Greek Anthology*
Zoshchenko, *Scenes from the Bathhouse*
Thrupp, *The Merchant Class of Medieval London*
Procopius, *Secret History*
Adcock, *Roman Political Ideas and Practice*
Swanson, *The Birth of the Gods*
Xenophon, *The March Up Country*
Trotsky, *The New Course*
Buchanan and Tullock, *The Calculus of Consent*
Hobson, *Imperialism*
Pobedonostsev, *Reflections of a Russian Statesman*
Kinietz, *The Indians of the Western Great Lakes 1615–1760*
Bromage, *Writing for Business*
Lurie, *Mountain Wolf Woman, Sister of Crashing Thunder*
Leonard, *Baroque Times in Old Mexico*
Meier, *Negro Thought in America, 1880–1915*
Burke, *The Philosophy of Edmund Burke*
Michelet, *Joan of Arc*
Conze, *Buddhist Thought in India*
Arberry, *Aspects of Islamic Civilization*
Chesnutt, *The Wife of His Youth and Other Stories*
Gross, *Sound and Form in Modern Poetry*
Zola, *The Masterpiece*
Chesnutt, *The Marrow of Tradition*
Aristophanes, *Four Comedies*
Aristophanes, *Three Comedies*

Chesnutt, *The Conjure Woman*
Duckett, *Carolingian Portraits*
Rapoport and Chammah, *Prisoner's Dilemma*
Aristotle, *Poetics*
Peattie, *The View from the Barrio*
Duckett, *Death and Life in the Tenth Century*
Langford, *Galileo, Science and the Church*
McNaughton, *The Taoist Vision*
Anderson, *Matthew Arnold and the Classical Tradition*
Milio, *9226 Kercheval*
Weisheipl, *The Development of Physical Theory in the Middle Ages*
Breton, *Manifestoes of Surrealism*
Gershman, *The Surrealist Revolution in France*
Lester, *Theravada Buddhism in Southeast Asia*
Scholz, *Carolingian Chronicles*
Marković, *From Affluence to Praxis*
Wik, *Henry Ford and Grass-roots America*
Sahlins and Service, *Evolution and Culture*
Wickham, *Early Medieval Italy*
Waddell, *The Wandering Scholars*
Rosenberg, *Bolshevik Visions* (2 parts in 2 vols.)
Mannoni, *Prospero and Caliban*
Aron, *Democracy and Totalitarianism*
Shy, *A People Numerous and Armed*
Taylor, *Roman Voting Assemblies*
Goodfield, *An Imagined World*
Hesiod, *The Works and Days; Theogony; The Shield of Herakles*
Raverat, *Period Piece*
Lamming, *In the Castle of My Skin*
Fisher, *The Conjure-Man Dies*
Strayer, *The Albigensian Crusades*
Lamming, *The Pleasures of Exile*
Lamming, *Natives of My Person*
Glaspell, *Lifted Masks and Other Works*
Wolff, *Aesthetics and the Sociology of Art*
Grand, *The Heavenly Twins*
Cornford, *The Origin of Attic Comedy*
Allen, *Wolves of Minong*
Brathwaite, *Roots*
Fisher, *The Walls of Jericho*
Lamming, *The Emigrants*
Loudon, *The Mummy!*
Kemble and Butler Leigh, *Principles and Privilege*
Thomas, *Out of Time*